Florida Lighthouses

30 Beacons and the Keepers Who Tended Them

Written by Rick and Terri Tuers

Foreword by James Hyland,
the Lighthouse Preservation Society

4880 Lower Valley Road • Atglen, PA 19310

OTHER SCHIFFER BOOKS BY THE AUTHOR:
Lighthouses of New York, ISBN 978-0-7643-2692-9

OTHER SCHIFFER BOOKS ON RELATED SUBJECTS:
Massachusetts Lighthouses and Lightships, Arthur P. Richmond, ISBN 978-0-7643-4853-2

Lighthouses: Maine to Florida, David Biggy, ISBN 978-0-7643-3177-0

Lighthouses and Coastal Attractions of Northern New England: New Hampshire, Maine, and Vermont, Allan Wood, ISBN 978-0-7643-5235-5

Copyright © 2019 by Rick and Terri Tuers
Library of Congress Control Number: 2019936852

All rights reserved. No part of this work may be reproduced or used in any form or by any means—graphic, electronic, or mechanical, including photocopying or information storage and retrieval systems—without written permission from the publisher.

The scanning, uploading, and distribution of this book or any part thereof via the Internet or any other means without the permission of the publisher is illegal and punishable by law. Please purchase only authorized editions and do not participate in or encourage the electronic piracy of copyrighted materials.

"Schiffer," "Schiffer Publishing, Ltd.," and the pen and inkwell logo are registered trademarks of Schiffer Publishing, Ltd.

Designed by Ashley Millhouse
Cover design by Jack Chappell

All photos courtesy of Rick and Terri Tuers unless otherwise noted
Type set in Arrus BT

ISBN: 978-0-7643-5873-9
Printed in China

Published by Schiffer Publishing, Ltd.
4880 Lower Valley Road
Atglen, PA 19310
Phone: (610) 593-1777; Fax: (610) 593-2002
E-mail: Info@schifferbooks.com
Web: www.schifferbooks.com

For our complete selection of fine books on this and related subjects, please visit our website at www.schifferbooks.com. You may also write for a free catalog.

Schiffer Publishing's titles are available at special discounts for bulk purchases for sales promotions or premiums. Special editions, including personalized covers, corporate imprints, and excerpts, can be created in large quantities for special needs. For more information, contact the publisher.

We are always looking for people to write books on new and related subjects. If you have an idea for a book, please contact us at proposals@schifferbooks.com.

Contents

Foreword 6

Acknowledgments. 11

1 | Introduction 12

2 | History of America's Lighthouses and the Administration 14

3 | Physics of Lighthouses: Lamps, Lenses, and Fuels 18

4 | East Coast Lights: Amelia Island to Cape Florida 25

5 | The Florida Keys: Fowey Rocks to Dry Tortugas 69

6 | West Coast Lights: Cedar Key to Sanibel Island 107

7 | Panhandle Lights: Pensacola to St. Marks 130

8 | Lost Beacons of Florida. 161

9 | Preserving Lighthouses and Maritime History in Florida and America. 177

Appendixes. 180

   Appendix 1: Maps, Guides, and Handbooks 180

   Appendix 2: Unique Florida Lighthouse Facts 181

Lighthouse Glossary. 182

Bibliography. 184

Index 186

Biographies of Rick and Terri Tuers. 190

LIST OF FIGURES

Figure 3-1. First-order Fresnel lens—cutaway
Figure 3-2. Light refraction in Fresnel lens
Figure 3-3. Fresnel lens dimensions
Figure 4-1. Explorers, settlements, and statehood timeline

LIST OF MAPS

Map 1. East Coast Lighthouses. 25
Map 2. Florida Keys Lighthouses 69
Map 3. West Coast Lighthouses 107
Map 4. Panhandle Lighthouses 130
Map 5. All Florida Lighthouses. 192

Dedication

We would like to dedicate this book to Jesus, who is the Light of the World. Without Him, this book would not have been possible. This book is also dedicated to Bodie, our dear fur-person, who traveled the shores of Florida while we photographed the lighthouses for this book.

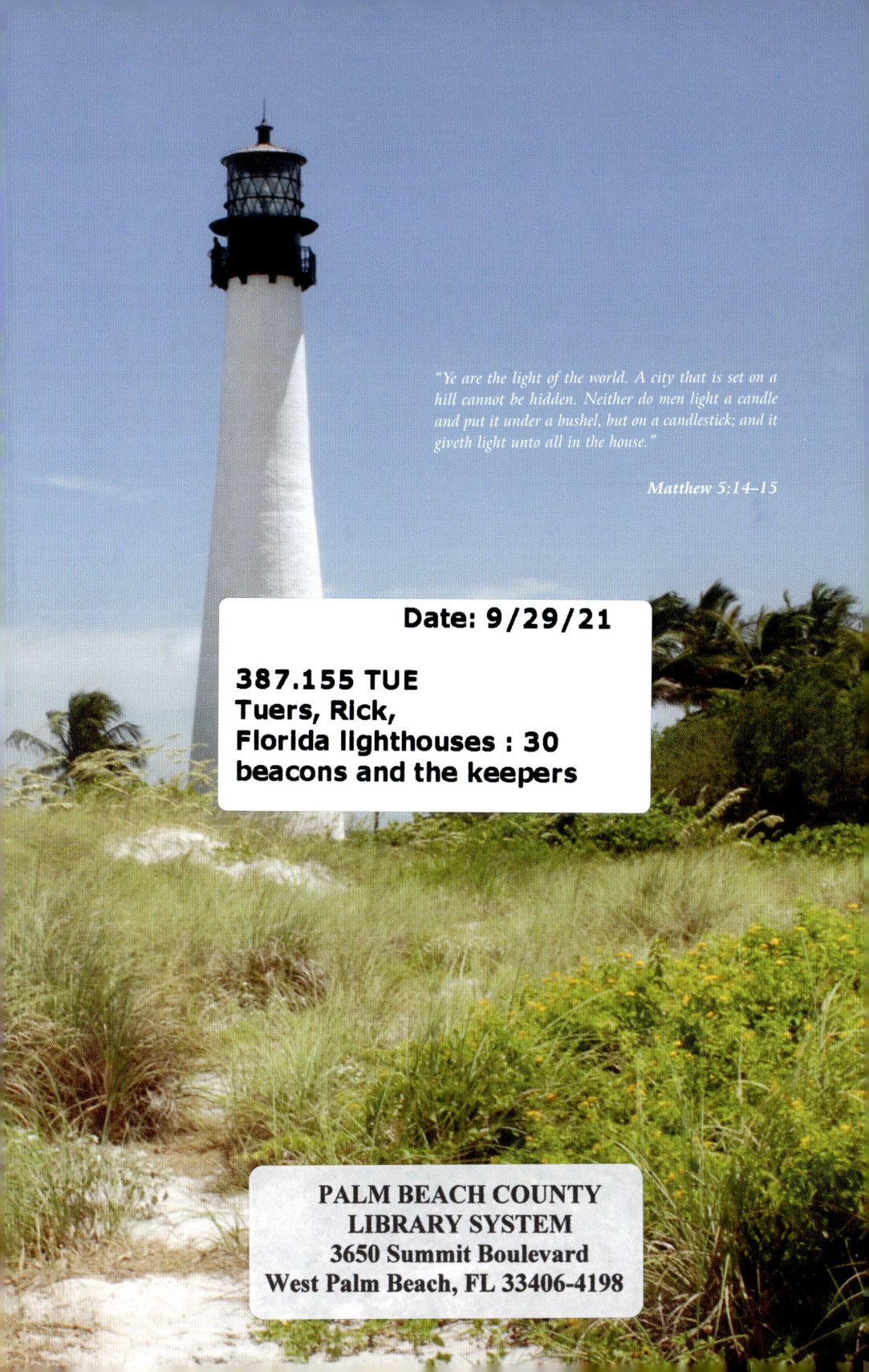

Foreword

A few years ago, I was descending a five-story lighthouse tower on a dark and stormy night. Our nonprofit organization offers romantic dinners at the top of the Newburyport Lighthouse as a fundraiser, and I had just cleaned up the lens room. I was proceeding downstairs with a tray full of dishes when the lights suddenly went out. Instantly, I froze in my tracks. It was pitch black, and I couldn't see a thing. It was like being in a cave. I tried to suppress the growing sense of panic I felt when I realized that one false move could send me headlong down the spiral staircase, or, worse yet, over the railing and down the open shaft of the tower, to my death, 50 feet below. Providentially, I remembered that I had a small electric candle that we used for the romantic dinner, and after switching it on I was able to carefully make my way down the dark staircase.

Eventually, we will all have the frightening experience of finding ourselves in an exceedingly dark place. Our fear of the dark goes back to our earliest childhood. It is what motivates parents to install nightlights in their children's bedrooms. Even as adults, we do our best to avoid dark places. But whether it's a familiar or unfamiliar location we find ourselves in, everything suddenly changes when the lights go out, and we find ourselves unable to get our bearings. When that happens, fear can begin to well up inside us as we desperately grope our way around, hoping to find the light switch, or the door out, in which to escape the pitch-dark, inky blackness unharmed.

It wasn't that long ago that the whole world lived in relative darkness once the sun went down. Fires, dimly lit candles, and oil lamps were the means by which mankind chased away the darkness. The invention of Thomas Edison's lightbulb changed the world dramatically, allowing us to brightly light up our homes, roads, and cities so we could travel around safely at night.

Now, imagine being a sailor on a boat without electric lights, one hundred years ago or more, on a stormy night in uncharted waters. Mountainous waves are flinging you violently, up and down and side to side. In the distance, above the shrieking winds, you hear the deadly thunder of waves crashing. Maddeningly, the sound is getting closer, but without any light, you can't get your bearings, so you don't know which way to turn. The growing dread you've felt for hours, since the storm began, now turns to wild terror as you realize that disaster is about to strike at any moment and you'll soon become food for sharks. Completely in the dark, with nothing but blackness all around, you're helpless to respond to the approaching danger. The boat is at the mercy of the wind and the waves and, like most sailors before the last

century, you don't know how to swim. As shipwreck threatens, you become paralyzed with an overwhelming fear as you helplessly anticipate your death.

Then, suddenly, a gleam of light flashes out over the waves! It gives you a quick glimpse of where you are. You've rounded a point and a lighthouse has appeared, sending out its sweeping rays of hope across the churning seas, finally giving you your bearings. Quickly, you realize your location. Deadly shoals lie straight ahead, but now you know how to steer clear of them. Suddenly, your fear vanishes, hope revives, and you jump into action. Because of the light, your salvation seems certain. You steer past the lighthouse and sail into safe harbor.

In 1839, a naval officer approaching a similar remote lighthouse on a stormy night wrote that "There are no words to express the feelings that induce a sailor to offer fervent prayers when he sees this mark of sympathy expressed by his fellow men. Suddenly he sees that he is no longer alone in the midst of the ocean waves: he sees that people are caring for him."

Until the turn of the last century, before there were good roads to travel or planes to fly, people and goods often traveled by water. Safety along our nation's waterways was therefore of the utmost importance. That's why our federal government lost no time in enacting the Lighthouse Act, which was the ninth Act of Congress and was signed into law by George Washington on August 7, 1789. It created the US Lighthouse Establishment under the Department of the Treasury, which was overseen by Alexander Hamilton. Because it was our nation's first public-works act, it has been called "the first great work of the American people." The goal was to create a system of beacons along our coastline so that a sailor would never be out of sight of a light. It made our shores among the safest in the world and created an impressive collection of over a thousand lighthouse structures—the largest number built by any nation in the world—with a large array of architectural styles, shapes, sizes, and colors. It was important that lighthouses looked different from each other so that they would not be confused with other towers.

Among the most spectacular of America's beacons are the lighthouses of Florida. Ranging from the open construction of offshore, wave-swept lights to the impressive masonry of tall towers, which were designed to be seen from far away in distant shipping lanes, Florida has one of the largest and most interesting collections of lighthouses of any state in America.

Foreword

No other state has a richer or more colorful maritime history. The early Spanish presence here, predating the other European settlements in the rest of the country by decades, brought amazing tales of Spanish galleons laden with riches, pirates, battles, buried and sunken treasures, hurricanes, shipwrecks, and heroic stories of rescues and survival. It is a truly unique history, filled with enough romance, harrowing adventure, and intrigue to easily capture the imagination.

Florida's romantic history, combined with its reputation for being a tropical paradise and vacation wonderland, is a big part of the draw for northerners—like myself—who, seeking escape from winter's ice and snow, make annual pilgrimages to its beautiful beaches. When visiting Florida, I always search out local lighthouses to photograph. Like exclamation points along the coast, these shoreline sentinels, often surrounded by palm trees, seem to capture the essence of the Florida coast.

The thirty lighthouses that dot the shores have played a vital role in Florida's vibrant maritime story. We should not take them for granted. I applaud all those who are diligently working to preserve these amazing structures for future generations.

The coauthor of this book, Rick Tuers, first became known to me several years ago in upstate New York at a slideshow lecture I had given on the need to preserve America's lighthouses. At the time, he was interested in writing a book about lighthouses and asked for any ideas on where to direct his research. Without hesitation, I suggested the lighthouses of New York State—no one had ever brought together the very diverse coastline of that unusual state, which included two Great Lakes, the Atlantic Ocean, the Saint Lawrence Seaway, Lake Champlain, and the Hudson River. It didn't take Rick long to take my advice and run with it, producing the most comprehensive book on what had been the biggest dark hole in American lighthouse history.

Now that Rick has moved to Florida, he has combined his considerable research and Terri's writing skills to document Florida's iconic lighthouses. Add to that his photographic skills, and you have a great recipe for a successful book. Knowing Terri and Rick's love for travel and adventure, the reader is in for an amazingly well-researched trip down the corridors of Florida's fascinating lighthouse history.

James Ward Hyland III
President/Founder
The Lighthouse Preservation Society

Acknowledgments

After relocating to Venice, Florida, in 2013, my wife and I contacted Schiffer Publishing in the spring of 2016 about *Florida Lighthouses*. In a state that is second only to Alaska in the number of miles of coastline, it made sense to write a book similar to our first published book, *Lighthouses of New York*.

It has taken over eighteen months to travel the entire state to shoot images and collect data for this book. Although I had visited a few of the East Coast lighthouses during our trips to Florida, I still needed to capture most of the images. We traveled extensively to shoot the ones in the Panhandle and the West Coast, and then we finished the East Coast. The Keys presented an entirely new challenge for us, since most are located offshore on fragile reefs.

We had to be creative since we do not own a boat or an airplane. To my surprise and delight, we were able to make contacts through the Florida Lighthouse Association, our Venice running group, and our church family to successfully tackle the job by sea and air. I had the privilege of flying in an experimental plane to shoot the Egmont and Anclote Key lighthouses. On another occasion, my wife and I flew in a private plane to photograph the lighthouses southeast of Miami down to Key West. Thanks to Paul and Marilyn Hollowell, we were able to make this exciting trip in two days. Special thanks go to Jamie Fraser for the West Coast flight from Venice up to the Tampa area. Both of these flights helped us immensely.

Other angels helped us in various ways. I would like to thank some key members of the Florida Lighthouse Association: Chris Belcher, president; Josh Liller; Richard Sanchez; Sharon McKenzie; and Neil Hurley, historian. I would also like to recognize Candace Clifford of the US Lighthouse Society (USLHS) and her gift of organizing and preparing USLHS archives. A special thank-you to Kelly Clark of the Dry Tortugas National Park, who assisted with the necessary permits to fly near the park. Many of the historical societies also gave me permission to enter the inner confines of the lighthouses and photograph areas that would otherwise be off-limits.

I am grateful for all those historians who have preserved the history of the lighthouses by storing artifacts in the National Archives, museums, public libraries, and historical societies. All the recorders of history, through their publications, have been instrumental in helping to weave the maritime history of Florida. Thank you, James Hyland, of the Lighthouse Preservation Society, for writing the foreword.

I credit my mom and dad for giving me my first camera when I was seven years old and nurturing my love of photography. Last, I would like to thank my wife, Terri, for her inspiration, her encouragement, and her meticulous and tireless dedication and assistance with the writing and editing. This book would not have been possible without her creative efforts.

CHAPTER 1:
Introduction

I have been in love with lighthouses for as long as I can remember. As a youngster growing up in Parsippany, New Jersey, I vacationed with my family in Seaside Heights, New Jersey, a small community on Barnegat Bay near Toms River. We fished off the pier, went crabbing in the bay, and spent days swimming, collecting shells, and walking the famous boardwalk. Eventually, I continued the summer tradition and brought my son there. Around 1980, I discovered F. Ross Holland's book *America's Lighthouses* and began to visit all the lighthouses in New Jersey, New York, Connecticut, and Massachusetts. For the past twenty years, I have been privileged to travel to nearly all the coastal states in America, including Hawaii and Alaska, and have photographed close to three hundred lighthouses.

After retiring in 2013 from the New York State Department of Environmental Conservation as coastal engineer, my wife and I relocated to Venice, Florida. Venice is a beautiful coastal Gulf community, located halfway between Tampa and Ft. Myers. Florida is second only to Alaska in the number of miles of coastline and beaches. With over 1,350 miles of coastline, Florida was the place to develop a book on lighthouses.

As Florida was explored and settled by the Spanish, there were many maritime challenges and wrecks on shoals and sandbars along its vast shoreline. Since the beginning of recorded history, over two thousand ships have wrecked off its coast. As early as 1569, the Spanish constructed simple wooden watchtowers that served as day markers. At Mosquito Inlet (today's Ponce Inlet), the British established the first documented, government-funded structure designed as a beacon or day marker. In 1774, Angelo Vackiere was the first keeper and was paid $24 per year for maintaining the beacon at Mosquito Inlet. The first American light station in Florida became operational in St. Augustine on April 5, 1824.

Currently, there are a total of thirty lighthouses in Florida. Not all of them operate as aids to navigation, but all remind us of the time before current technologies such as radar, sonar, radio beacons, and depth finders were regularly used tools to navigate.

Florida Lighthouses is a collection of photos and information on each current beacon. The book is organized by regions, starting with the East Coast and then traveling down to the Keys, around the West Coast, and up along the Panhandle. There is a brief history of the Lighthouse Service, which stemmed from the

Introduction

Dames Point (1876). One of the only river lighthouses in Florida, it was preceded by a lightship. *Courtesy of the US Coast Guard*

Lighthouse Establishment, established by George Washington in August 1789. The chapter "Physics of Lighthouses—Lamps, Lenses, and Fuels" explains the design of the Fresnel lens and takes you through the history of how lighthouses were fueled. A chapter featuring many findings on the lost beacons and lightships of Florida add to the rich maritime history. Complementing *Florida Lighthouses* are sidebars on the intricacies of architecture and construction, dedicated lighthouse keepers, and notable assassins imprisoned off the coast of Key West. Sit back, relax, and enjoy this collection of stories about a vital and colorful part of Florida's history.

Jupiter Inlet. The tower walls are 31.5 inches thick at the base and taper to 18 inches at the top.

CHAPTER 2:
History of America's Lighthouses and the Administration

FIRST LIGHTHOUSES IN AMERICA

The first lighthouses in America were constructed to safely navigate between Boston, New York, and Philadelphia. After America was colonized, trade routes were established, and maps were made on the basis of captains' logbooks. Shallow sandbars, reefs, or rock outcrops were often found by accident. The lessons learned were capitalized on by placing markers and updating navigation maps.

It is believed that the tower erected on Little Brewster Island in Boston Harbor in 1716 was the first North American lighthouse. This lighthouse was blown up during the Revolutionary War and later rebuilt in 1783. However, there is some evidence that an earlier lighthouse was built in Havana, Cuba, in 1671. Other historians site Fort Niagara (1782) as one of the earliest lighthouses in North America.

Definitively naming which light was the first in North America is not as important as knowing that American colonial lighthouses were built by states through taxes and lotteries. The Boston Lighthouse was followed by Brant Point, Massachusetts (1746); Beavertail, Rhode Island (1749); New London Harbor, Connecticut (1760); Sandy Hook, New Jersey (1764); Cape Henlopen, Delaware (1765); Charleston, South Carolina (1767); Plymouth, Massachusetts (1768); Portsmouth, New Hampshire (1771); Cape Ann, Massachusetts (1771); Great Point, Massachusetts (1784); and Newbury, Massachusetts (1788).

EARLY ADMINISTRATION

President George Washington was a big promoter of lighthouses. In 1789, he urged Congress to recognize lighthouse construction as a national priority. Congress responded by passing its ninth piece of legislation on August 7, 1789, creating the Lighthouse Establishment, which later became the Lighthouse Service. Congress assigned the aids to navigation to the Department of the Treasury under Alexander Hamilton. Presidents Washington, Adams, and Jefferson personally approved the construction contracts for lighthouses. They also appointed and dismissed lighthouse keepers. In 1792, Hamilton assigned this responsibility to the Commissioner of Revenue.

LIGHTHOUSE SERVICE'S FIRST PROJECTS

When the Lighthouse Service was in its infancy, the number of lighthouses in operation was very small. To remedy this, a major construction program added a dozen lighthouses by the end of the eighteenth century. Lighthouses were completed or started at Cape Henry, Virginia (1791); Portland Head, Maine (1791); Tybee, Georgia (1791); Sequin, Maine (1795); Bald Island, North Carolina (1796); Montauk Point, New York (1797); Baker's Island, Massachusetts (1798); Cape Cod, Massachusetts (1798); Cape Hatteras, North Carolina (1798); Ocracoke, North Carolina (1798); Gay Head, Massachusetts (1798); and Eatons Neck, New York (1799).

This initial burst of construction was nearly complete when President George Washington died in 1799. Washington's insistence that lighthouse construction was made a national priority helped create a more effective approach to manage and construct lighthouses along America's East Coast.

FIFTH AUDITOR (1820)

In 1802, Albert Gallatin, the secretary of the Treasury, resumed responsibility for the lighthouses. This was shifted back in 1813 to the commissioner of revenue. In 1820, Stephen Pleasonton, a hardworking auditor, became the fifth auditor of America's lighthouses. He remained at his post for nearly forty years and was known as the general superintendent of lighthouses. By 1842, the Lighthouse Establishment consisted of 256 lighthouses and thirty floating lightships. As general superintendent, he kept very tight control over the activities of the local superintendents. Because Pleasonton had very little nautical background, he relied on the professional experience of Winslow Lewis. Pleasonton prided himself on that fact that for many years, he was able to return funds appropriated for construction and repairs unspent. He also took great pride in his record of running the American lighthouses at less than one-half the cost at which the Trinity House operated the English lighthouses. Many lighthouses constructed during this period were done by the lowest bidder. Most of the time, these inferior structures constantly needed to be repaired or replaced. Many complaints about the quality of the lights followed.

US LIGHTHOUSE BOARD (1852)

Matters were getting worse. In 1847, Congress took action by taking away the construction of the lighthouses from the fifth auditor and placed it under the Army Corps of Engineers. In 1851, Congress authorized an investigating board consisting of two high-ranking naval officers, two officers from the Army Corps of Engineers, a civilian scientist, and a junior officer of the navy. In 1852, a 750-page report critical of the fifth auditor was presented to Congress. Many of the seamen's testimony said that "they could not distinguish between the different lighthouses." This meant that the lighting apparatus—the reflector-type lamps that Winslow Lewis had recommended—was obsolete. Congress proposed that a Lighthouse Board be created. It first met on October 9, 1852, at which time Commodore William Shubrick and his nine-member board had a huge job ahead of them to modernize all the lighthouses.

To begin with, the country was divided into twelve districts, and the president assigned an army or naval officer as an inspector for each district. The Lighthouse Board moved quickly to install Fresnel lenses, which were successfully used in European lighthouses. The board created central depots, such as Staten Island and Buffalo, to assist with inventory, dispatch, and repair of equipment. Over the next fifty years, the board was mindful of advancing technologies and worked to install new types of lighthouses, buoys, and fog signals. Several of the new technologies included the development of screw-pile lighthouses, skeleton lighthouses, wave-swept interlocking lighthouses, iron caisson lighthouses, and breakwater lighthouses. Several advances in fog signals included fog whistles, mechanically run clockworks, steam boiler whistles, steam boiler reed-trumpets, and bell signals. In 1886, a new technology was tested to illuminate the Statue of Liberty by using electricity.

LIGHTHOUSE BUREAU (1910)

In 1910, Congress wanted to give a civilian presence to the administration, abolished the US Lighthouse Board, and created the Lighthouse Bureau under the Department of Commerce. The board hired a number of experienced civilians that took over the roles that the military officers had been fulfilling. President Taft appointed George R. Putnam to head the new agency as the commissioner of the Lighthouse Bureau. For twenty-five years, Putnam effectively led the bureau, and the number of aids to navigation increased substantially from 11,713 to 24,000. The increased aids were mostly buoys and small lights. In 1916, a device was developed to automatically replace burned-out electric lamps, along with the first experimental radio beacon the following year. In 1928, the first automated radio beacon was installed. With the installation of more automated lights, the Lighthouse Bureau staff was reduced by eight hundred employees.

By the 1920s and '30s, the majority of the lighthouses had electric service, reducing the staff to operate the stations. In 1933, a photoelectric alarm device was developed to check the operation of unmanned lights, and in 1934 a remote-controlled lightship was equipped by the Lighthouse Bureau.

COAST GUARD

On July 7, 1939, the Lighthouse Bureau was merged with the US Coast Guard. Former bureau personnel were given the choice to remain civilians, but about half chose to become members of the Coast Guard. During World War II, one of the many jobs of the Coast Guard was to guard the shores of the country. With the help of volunteers and career Coast Guard personnel, the Beach Patrol was formed to guard against enemy invasion, rescuing victims of German submarine warfare and retrieving drowning victims. Some of the new technologies developed by the Coast Guard during and after World War II were radio technologies called SHORAN (short-range navigation aids) and LORAN (long-range navigation aids). By the end of World War II, the Coast Guard staffed 468 light stations.

In 1962, there were still 327 manned stations, despite the Coast Guard's effort to remove keepers from isolated stations. In 1968, they initiated the Lighthouse Automation and Modernization Program (LAMP). The LAMP program was designed to accelerate and standardize the remaining lighthouses for automation. Over $26 million was spent on LAMP over twenty years, running through 1989. The estimated annual savings from automating the lighthouses was about seven million dollars. By 1990, all lighthouses but one, the Boston Harbor Island in Massachusetts, were automated.

The Coast Guard soon encountered a rising grassroots concern over the preservation of these old light stations, and many historical societies expressed a strong interest in obtaining a lighthouse to preserve and keep open to the public. The Coast Guard set up a process for leasing the stations to local historical groups. Many of the preservation groups that were successful in preserving lighthouses were given ownership of a lighthouse and its surrounding property.

CHAPTER 3:
Physics of Lighthouses: Lamps, Lenses, and Fuels

The technologies used in the design and construction of lighthouses were part of an evolutionary process that began in the Industrial Revolution. Many design processes developed during the industrial age assisted engineers, architects, and contractors in building the lighthouses throughout America. Several styles of fuel-burning lamps were patented prior to the discovery of petroleum in Pennsylvania. Augustin Jean Fresnel then designed a glass prism lens that focused and brilliantly magnified light, transforming the lighthouse community.

EARLY LIGHTS

The first lighthouses, which predated those in America, used wood as a fuel. For almost two thousand years, wood was the only source of light for lighthouses. These lights were probably perched on a hillside that faced seaward. Towers were constructed and wood fires were placed on top. Around the beginning of the sixteenth century, when coal was discovered in Europe, it was used for fuel because it produced a light that the sailors preferred. Experiments were done with candles, but the light given off was not as bright as that from coal. As early as 1759 in England, the Eddystone Lighthouse used an oil lamp that contained a flat wick. One of the shortcomings of this new lamp was the light smoke it gave off, which created a haze over the glass interior of the lantern room. A lantern with a pan and four wicks was an improvement made in the 1790s that met with limited success. This lamp type was used in the Boston Lighthouse as the principal illuminant until 1812.

ARGAND LAMP WITH REFLECTORS

The first major breakthrough in illumination was a design that was perfected by Swiss chemist Aimé Argand (born in Geneva, Switzerland, in 1750; died in Geneva in 1803). The Argand lamp burned oil in a wick between two concentric tubes, producing a circular flame with two sources of oxygen. A glass chimney provided constant air flow and protected the flame from irregular breezes. This lamp burned more intensely and was smokeless, and the flame was equivalent to seven candles. In England, 18-to-20-inch reflectors were fitted to the Argand lamp. This lamp achieved a pinnacle of success in England and France.

Later, it was adopted by Augustin Fresnel for the lamps used in his lenses. In 1810, Captain Winslow Lewis persuaded the American federal government to adopt the Argand lamp with parabolic reflectors. His rationale was that these lamps gave off a brighter light and used about one-half as much oil. Lewis patented his lamp system and offered to sell the patent to the government. He proposed to outfit all forty-nine lighthouses for a sum of $26,950.

Unfortunately, right from beginning, these lamps were inferior. It was noted by inspectors and keepers that the silver finish on the reflectors or mirrors easily wore off. During the review by Stephen Pleasonton, the fifth auditor, he never identified this as problem to the Lighthouse Service. These practices did not begin to change until the Lighthouse Service was created in 1851.

THE FRESNEL STORY

Soon after the formation of the federal government, the US Treasury Department became responsible for the early management of the lighthouse system. The secretary of the Treasury personally administered lighthouses for several years, but due to growing commerce, lighthouse operations required more time. As a result, the commissioner of revenue handled day-to-day management until 1802.

Several transfers of responsibility took place between 1802 and 1820. It shifted between the secretary of the Treasury and the commissioner of revenue. In 1820, the lighthouse system became the responsibility of the fifth auditor of the Treasury, Stephen Pleasonton. The lighthouse system at that time consisted of 256 lighthouses, thirty floating lights, and a substantial number of beacons and buoys. Pleasonton appointed local supervisors who handled all personnel matters, inspections, repairs to lighthouses, and expenditures.

Original First-order Fresnel lens—Cape May, New Jersey. *Authors' collection*

THE FRESNEL LENS

In 1822 Augustin Jean Fresnel (fray-NEL), a French physicist, introduced his magnification invention that would change the world. The lens is shaped like a giant beehive that surrounds a single lamp, consisting of curved leaded-glass prisms that are supported by a brass framework and are arranged to apply the lenticular principles of physics. By positioning the prisms around the outside of the lens so that all the emerging rays are parallel to each other, the lens is capable of collecting 90 percent of the lamp's light and concentrating it into an intense horizontal ray. The lamp was designed in different sizes known as "orders." The largest Fresnel lens is a "First-order" lens. First-order lenses were reserved primarily for tall coastal lighthouses, such as Jupiter Inlet. Fixed lenses could be made to flash by placing moving screens known as eclipsers in front of the optic. Some of the larger lenses were divided into separate halves known as bivalve or clamshell lenses. Figure 3-3 is a chart defining the dimensions of seven different orders of Fresnel lenses.

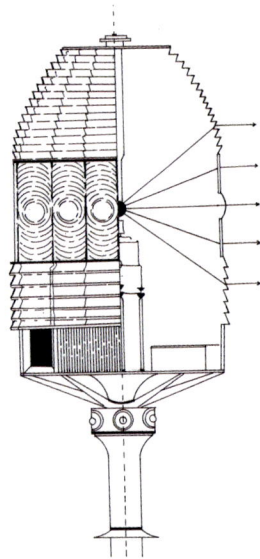

Figure 3-1. First-order Fresnel lens—cutaway. *Courtesy of C. Garretson-Persans*

The administration had a variety of problems, including Pleasonton's lack of technical and maritime experience. One example of Pleasonton's lack of insight was the time he wrote to France to inquire about the Fresnel lens. After being informed of the cost of these lenses, he decided that they were too expensive and they were not installed. Consequently, lighthouses in the United States did not meet other countries' standards. In 1838, inspections were made on the entire lighthouse system. After the study, Congress passed an act in 1838 that divided the Atlantic Coast into six districts and the Great Lakes into two districts. Each district was inspected by a naval officer, who also found that the lights were unsatisfactory. Some of the worst conditions were due to substandard construction materials or techniques. Lightships were also in poor condition. Unfortunately, no action was taken by Congress for many years. Due to criticism in the 1840s, Pleasonton and his lighthouse system came under investigation again in 1851. Starting in 1847, all newly constructed lighthouses were placed under the review of the Corps of Engineers.

Physics of Lighthouses: Lamps, Lenses, and Fuels

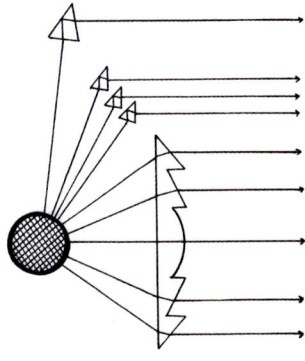

ORDER	HEIGHT	INSIDE DIAMETER
First	7' 10"	6' 1"
Second	6' 1"	4' 7"
Third	4' 8"	3' 3"
Third & one half	3' 0"	2' 5"
Fourth	2' 4"	1' 8"
Fifth	1' 8"	1' 3"
Sixth	1' 5"	1' 0"

Figure 3-2. Light refraction in Fresnel lens. *Courtesy of C. Garretson-Persans*

Figure 3-3. Fresnel lens dimensions

Today, the Coast Guard maintains nine active landfall First-order Fresnel lenses on the Atlantic Coast, four of which are in Florida. They are located at St. Augustine, Jupiter Inlet, Pensacola, and Ponce Inlet. Depending on the weather, a First-order lens that is positioned at a height of 100 feet is visible for up to 18 miles. These lenses could consist of up to a thousand prisms, are up to 12 feet tall, weigh over 3 tons, and are valued at approximately $1 million apiece. There is a wonderful collection of Fresnel lenses at Ponce Inlet Lighthouse.

Four years later, Congress appointed a committee to investigate the operation of several governmental departments and make recommendations. The committee decided to remove lighthouse duties from the fifth auditor and reassign them to the commissioner of revenue. Congress authorized and required several civilian, naval, and army engineers to investigate the entire lighthouse system. This included construction, management, lighting, efficiency, and comparing the American system to that of other countries. Their findings also concluded that many lighthouses were poorly spaced. There were reports from seamen who could not see or distinguish between lights. Many lighthouses and lightships were defective. Training for keepers needed to be revamped, since many were either unqualified or incompetent. The investigators also found a poor distribution of supplies. The board proposed a complete revamping of the system, which included adding Fresnel lenses in all new and existing lighthouses.

OTHER FUELS

The early American lighthouses used whale oil as a fuel. There were two strains of fuel used, depending on the time of year. A thick strain, known as summer oil, was used in the warmer months, while a thinner one was used in winter. In colder climates during the winter, the thin oil tended to solidify, and it became necessary to keep a warming stove in the lantern room to maintain the proper viscosity. Sperm oil was used because it provided a high-quality bright light. In 1855, sperm oil cost $2.25 per gallon, which had increased from fifty-five cents a gallon in 1840.

The Lighthouse Service began to look for a cheaper fuel. The French were using colza and rapeseed oil, which were one-half the price of sperm oil. Rapeseed oil was obtained from wild cabbage. The government hoped to create a market, but the farmers did not grow a sufficient quantity to fill the needs of the Lighthouse Service. In the 1850s, they began to use colza oil. Within a few years, this supply was also insufficient.

A committee led by John Henry of the Smithsonian Institution tested lard oil. Previous efforts had resulted in failure, but the new tests of the oil showed that if the oil was heated to a higher temperature, it burned well. By 1867, lard oil was used exclusively in larger lamps. In the 1870s, tests were done with kerosene or mineral oil. The tests were successful, and in 1878 the board introduced this to Fourth-order and smaller lenses.

LAMPS

The next change was in the source of the light—the incandescent vapor lamp. This lamp is similar to the Coleman lamp used by campers today. With the vapor lamp, the kerosene is forced into a vaporizer chamber, where it strikes the hot walls and is instantly changed into a vapor. The vapors go through a series of small holes to the mantle, where it burns like a brilliant gas ball.

The final refinement was the testing of electricity around 1900. This was first used at the Statue of Liberty. In the 1920s and 1930s, generators were gradually introduced where power lines did not reach. When lighthouses used electricity or timer switches were installed, a keeper was not necessary. Multiple bulb holders were another invention that automated lighthouses. A multiple bulb holder automatically moved a new bulb to replace a burned-out one. As one can see, there were many factors that led to the extinction of the lighthouse keeper's role.

LIGHTHOUSE GENERALS

In 1852, experienced military officers, engineers, and seamen took charge of the Lighthouse Service. The service immediately embarked on an ambitious program to expand and upgrade the navigation aids in America. Because the American economy was booming, Congress cooperated and provided funds to make these improvements. To accomplish these tasks, the Lighthouse Service relied on the skills of two young military engineers, George Meade and Danville Leadbetter.

George Meade was trained as an engineer and graduated from West Point in 1835 at the age of twenty. He was a surveyor for the Army Corps of Topographical Engineers and helped set the boundary between the United States and the Republic of Texas. Meade had an interest in marine engineering and lighthouses and began to work on towers in the Delaware Bay. Eventually Meade helped design several lighthouses in the Florida Keys: Carysfort Reef (1850), Sand Key, and Sombrero Key.

Danville Leadbetter, an 1836 graduate of West Point, built lighthouses in the Gulf of Mexico. He preferred to use brick but also designed steel skeleton towers. In 1858, he completed a 200-foot-tall tower at Sand Island off Alabama's Mobile Bay. Leadbetter oversaw the construction of Port Pontchartrain, built on a submerged concrete pad. His most unusual design was at Sabine Pass, which was supported with a fin link foundation that spread weight over a larger area. This tower was built on damp, yielding ground but has remained in place for over 150 years.

With the outbreak of the Civil War in 1861, Meade rose quickly through the ranks to general in the Union army. A string of key defeats of the Union Army of the Potomac had President Lincoln fire many generals. Meade was moved into this position on the eve of the critical battle of Gettysburg. Because of Meade's experience in Florida, where he built structures that could withstand storms, Meade built his defense on a series of hills overlooking Gettysburg. On the third and final day of the battle, when Lee commanded the thirteen thousand troops of Pickett's charge, he maintained his position.

Leadbetter, joining the Confederate side, was in charge of Gulf Coast fortifications and lighthouses. Because the Confederate naval force was weak, under Leadbetter's direction the Southern troops carefully removed and hid the Fresnel lenses to keep them out of the hands of the enemy. During the war, some key lighthouses were blown up. One such target was the Sand Island lighthouse, which Leadbetter had built only a few years earlier.

CHAPTER 4:
East Coast Lights: Amelia Island to Cape Florida

NATIVE FLORIDIANS, EXPLORATION, COLONIZATION, AND STATEHOOD OF FLORIDA

Florida's history extends back sixteen centuries. The first Floridians hunted animals different from those found today: bison, camels, mastodons, and mammoths. The first permanent settlements by Native Americans were established around 5000 BCE along the St. Johns River on the East Coast and on the West Coast near Tampa. Archeologists have discovered that around 2000 BCE, Native American tribes made fired-clay pottery. By 500 BCE, there were many established tribes throughout the peninsula, including the Timucua, the Calusa, and the Apalachee. The Ais lived near the Indian River, the Creeks and Choctaws in the Panhandle, the Matecumbe in the Florida Keys, and the Tequesta in southeastern Florida. The population estimates vary widely; however, by the time the Europeans arrived, there were between 100,000 and 300,000 people in Florida.

In 1513, Juan Ponce de León visited both coasts of Florida as he explored the New World. On March 3, 1513, his three ships sailed north, and on April 2 they sighted land. He named the cape "Cape Canaveral," the first European name for a point in North America. He claimed it for the king of Spain and named the territory La Florida, "feast of flowers," because it was the Easter season. On his second voyage in 1521, he brought two hundred settlers, both men and women, along with farming implements, plants, and animals. As the Spanish left their ships somewhere near Port Charlotte, they were attacked three times. Ponce de León was shot with an arrow in his thigh. He ordered a retreat to Cuba, where he died from the poisonous arrow. Florida was visited, battled over, and settled by the Spanish, French, and English. Over three hundred years later, in 1819, Secretary of State John Quincy Adams acquired Florida from Spain.

Figure 4-1 shows a list of explorers who landed in Florida. Each of these explorers played an important role in the rich cultural history of early Florida. This history includes the building of forts and missions and establishing communities such as St. Augustine, which is the oldest city in America. Andrew Jackson was Florida's first territorial governor. In 1821, Monroe offered Jackson the governorship and Jackson resigned from the army. In 1847, Florida became the twenty-seventh state in America.

DATE	COUNTRY	EXPLORER/ SETTLEMENT	LOCATION
1513	Spain	Juan Ponce de Leon	Melborne Beach
1521	Spain	Juan Ponce de Leon	West Coast
1528	Spain	Painfilo de Narvaez	Tampa Bay
1539	Spain	Hernando de Soto	Tampa Bay
1562	French	John Ribault	St. John's River
1564	French	Rene de Laudonniere	St. Augustine
1565	Spain	Pedro Menendez de Aviles	St. Augustine
1568	French	Dominic de Gourgues	San Mateo
1573	Spain	Nombre de Dios	St. Augustine
1672	Spain	Castillo de San Marcos	St. Augustine
1717	French	Fort Crevecoeur	Beacon Hill
1719	French	—	Pensacola
1819	Spain	State of Florida	—
1845	—	State of Florida	—

Figure 4-1 Explorers, settlements, and statehood timeline

East Coast Lights: Amelia Island to Cape Florida

Amelia Island. Completed in 1839, it is the oldest existing lighthouse in Florida.

AMELIA ISLAND
(1820, 1839)

At the southern end of a chain of barrier islands (Sea Islands) stretching from South Carolina to Florida sits the crown jewel of Amelia Island—the Amelia Island Lighthouse. Amelia Island was named after the daughter of King George II of England. Located at the northern end of this historic barrier island, it is the oldest lighthouse in Florida. It is on the Florida-Georgia border in the northeastern part of the state, at the head of the St. Marys River Inlet, near Georgia's Cumberland Sound and the Fernandina Beach Harbor.

Amelia Island. This historical photo shows the lighthouse in 1880. *Courtesy of US Coast Guard*

Originally, this lighthouse was named the Little Cumberland Island Light, since it was located on Georgia's Little Cumberland Island. Planning for this coastal light began in 1819 by Winslow Lewis (1770–1850), a former sea captain who had numerous contracts to build lighthouses on the East Coast of America. He designed a 50-foot tower and a keeper's home on the southernmost barrier island in Georgia. Construction was completed and the lighthouse was lit in July 1820.

When the Lighthouse Service decided to build a taller lighthouse on the northern part of Little Cumberland Island, this lighthouse was dismantled and was moved across the channel to Amelia Island, where it still stands. Reconstruction was completed in 1839, making it the oldest and northernmost lighthouse in the state. The tower is made of red brick, which is painted white. It contains sixty-nine granite steps mined and transported by ship from New England. Originally Amelia was 50 feet tall but became 64 feet tall when a glistening black lantern was added in 1881. Although it is one of the shorter coastal lights on the East Coast, its focal plane is 107 feet above sea level.

When it was built, it contained an Argand lamp, which is a type of oil lamp that was invented and patented by Aimé Argand in 1780. This particular lamp had fourteen lamps, each with a 14-inch reflector. In 1858, it was replaced by a Third-order Fresnel lens. The lamp originally burned whale oil, and then kerosene. It was electrified in 1930. Amelia Island Lighthouse is a classic Victorian structure, but the lighthouse keeper's two-story home is keeping in line with the antebellum architecture of the homes on the island.

The US Coast Guard transferred ownership to the city of Fernandina Beach in 2001. It is maintained as a historical monument and is opened to visitors only on a limited basis. Since the lighthouse is closely surrounded by private homes, the city buses visitors to the site. Tour information can be found on the lighthouse website or through the Amelia Island Chamber of Commerce.

East Coast Lights: Amelia Island to Cape Florida

St. Johns River. It was constructed to 1859 and turned over to the navy in 1969. The current light is the third one at this location.

ST. JOHNS RIVER
(1830, 1835, 1859)

At 310 miles long, the St. Johns River is the longest river in the state of Florida. It snakes through swamplands of central Florida to the Atlantic Ocean. It is one of the few rivers in the United States that actually flows northward. Used both for commercial and recreational purposes, it winds through or borders twelve counties. The entrance to the St. Johns River has challenged mariners since the early days of exploration. The ocean and river meet at Mayport, the site of the French settlement begun by the Huguenot Jean Ribault in 1565.

At the mouth of the St. Johns River sits a decommissioned lighthouse, the St. Johns River Light. It is located on the grounds of the Mayport Naval Station in Jacksonville, Florida, and can be accessed only by the Florida Lighthouse Association.

The first light was built in 1830 where the present south jetty is located. It was one of the first aids to navigation in what was then the territory of Florida. It cost the government $24,000 and lasted only five years. In 1835, it was undermined by severe erosion. It was torn down and a second lighthouse was constructed a mile inland. This lighthouse was a conical tower, made of bricks and painted white. While it was thought to be safe from the forces of nature, this was not the case. By the 1850s, the shifting sands and the meandering river nearly buried the tower with large dunes, which made it much more difficult for boats to see the light.

When it could no longer be seen from the sea, the light was abandoned, and a third lighthouse was constructed in 1859. It was officially lit on August 1, 1859. This lighthouse stood 60 feet tall and contained a Third-order Fresnel lens. During the Civil War, like most lighthouses up and down the eastern coastline, this lighthouse was extinguished. The oil and the lighthouse fixtures were transported to Palatka and then Iola, Florida, for safekeeping. Following the Civil War, the US Lighthouse Board determined that the St. Johns Light was in need of extensive repair. A new cupola raised the tower to height of 81 feet, and a Third-order lens was added. The lighthouse was relit on July 1, 1867.

The lighthouse was deactivated in 1929 and was replaced by St. Johns Lightship off Mayport. In 1954, the navy replaced the lightship with a stronger beacon (Mayport Lighthouse) on the eastern end of the naval base. The Coast Guard turned over the old lighthouse to the navy in 1969, and some restoration work was done on the tower. In 1982, the St. Johns River Light was placed on the National Register of Historic Places.

St. Johns River / Mayport. Constructed of concrete, this light is similar to Egmont Lighthouse.

ST. JOHNS LIGHT STATION
(1954)

After the St. Johns Lightship was phased out, the St. Johns Light Station was the primary aid to navigation on the bustling St. Johns River. The modern concrete tower was built on a beach dune, about three-quarters of a mile south of the jetty. It took fourteen months to build at a cost of $250,000.

This is the newest of all Florida lighthouses and is located 1.8 miles south of the St. Johns River on the Mayport Naval Station. Only a mile from the St. Johns Lighthouse (old Mayport) and north of Jacksonville Beach, this lighthouse stands 64 feet tall and is 80 feet above sea level. This modern, art deco–styled structure is made of concrete and is similar to the Egmont Key Lighthouse near St. Petersburg.

It has an aero beacon of 200,000 candlepower that guides ships 22 nautical miles out in the Atlantic. It flashes white and red. In addition to guiding boats and ships with its beam, it also had a radio beacon, which is less expensive for pleasure boats to use than LORAN or radar. Radio beacons send out a Morse code, which boat captains use to determine their location. Today, radio beacons have been replaced by the global positioning system (GPS). This lighthouse also serves as a weather station.

St. Johns River / Mayport. Constructed in 1954, it is the newest lighthouse at this location.

East Coast Lights: Amelia Island to Cape Florida

St. Augustine. The barber-pole day markings resemble the Cape Hatteras Light, North Carolina.

ST. AUGUSTINE
(1842, 1848, 1852, 1874)

St. Augustine is the oldest city in Florida, and its lighthouse is equally rich in history. Pedro Menéndez de Avilés, a Spanish admiral and the first governor of Florida, founded the city of St. Augustine on September 8, 1565. Since this area was first sited on August 28, 1565, the feast day of St. Augustine, the city was named after the saint. Spanish architecture and Catholic influences can be seen throughout this beautiful, historic city.

St. Augustine was the first lighthouse established in Florida by the new territorial American government in 1824. Prior to this, explorer Menéndez ordered that several blockhouses be built along Florida's coastline to protect this Spanish settlement from natives and other explorers. He erected a 35-foot watchtower in 1585 on the northern end of Anastasia Island to protect the inlet and harbor. This watchtower was the predecessor of the current St. Augustine Lighthouse.

In 1821, Florida seceded to the United States. By 1824, under the orders of George Washington, the St. Augustine Lighthouse was constructed 1,000 feet southwest of the Spanish compound. Stephen Pleasanton, who was responsible for constructing and maintaining lighthouses throughout the United States, was the designer. The first lighthouse was completed in 1842 and was 30 feet tall. It was made of brick and was square in shape. Juan Andreu, the first keeper, was appointed on April 5, 1824. Andreu was a ship's pilot and was well acquainted with navigation in and out of this port. He tended ten whale oil lamps with silver 14-inch reflectors.

In 1848, the tower was built higher and reached 40 feet. In 1855, Joseph Andreu, the son of Juan Andreu, was appointed keeper, and lard oil was used in conjunction with a Fourth-order Fresnel lens. This lens provided a much more powerful light. In 1852, the tower was raised again to 52 feet.

On September 5, 1859, Joseph Andreu fell to his death when the scaffolding he was using to paint the lighthouse gave way. His wife, Maria de los Dolores Mestre Andreu, succeeded him. Replacing a keeper with his spouse was a common practice in those days. Spouses learned the trade alongside their husbands. As long as they were capable of carrying heavy containers of oil up to the lantern room, they could continue in their assignment. In 1866, the lighthouse keeper's home was completed. It was designed by James Renwick, the same architect who designed the Smithsonian Institution in Washington, DC, and St. Patrick's Cathedral in New York City.

During the Civil War, like most lighthouses on the East Coast, St. Augustine was taken out of commission. Mrs. Andreu helped the mayor of St. Augustine remove the lighthouse apparatus and bury the lens. When the Union gained control of St. Augustine, the mayor was thrown in prison for a time until he confessed the location of the lens. The lens was replaced in the lighthouse but remained off until it was put back into service in 1867.

In 1885, keepers began to use kerosene to fuel the lamp. On August 31, 1886, an unprecedented event took place. The lighthouse keeper recorded an earthquake, which was very uncommon to Florida. The 7.6 magnitude quake struck Charleston, South Carolina, at 2:00 a.m. It was felt as far away as Cuba and Bermuda. Thankfully, no damage was done to the lighthouse.

Erosion was a huge problem for this light. Authorities realized the changes in the coastline and the damage that grueling storms made on the tower. In 1871, 5 acres of land was purchased one-half mile from the old lighthouse, and $60,000 was appropriated for a new lighthouse to be built. Construction began using brick and coquina as a building material for the walls. On October 15, 1874, a First-order Fresnel lens was lit, which could be seen 19 miles into the Atlantic. Luckily, this light was finished before the original lighthouse fell into the sea on August 22, 1880. Evidence of the first tower exists as a submerged archeological site.

Ironically, the St. Augustine lighthouse is not located on the mainland in the city of St. Augustine, but on the eastern coast of Anastasia Island, a short distance south of the St. Augustine Inlet and downtown area. This striking structure, with its black-and-white barber-pole day markings, is 165 feet tall and is conical in shape. It closely resembles the Cape Hatteras lighthouse in North Carolina. Two hundred nineteen steps lead visitors to the lantern area, where a First-order Fresnel lens still flashes a fixed white light every thirty seconds. This lens consists of 370 hand-cut glass prisms arranged in a beehive shape towering 12 feet tall and 6 feet in diameter. Today it is lit by a 1,000-watt bulb that is maintained by the museum.

St. Augustine was the last Florida lighthouse to be electrified (1936). As World War II began, the threat of German U-boats on the East Coast of the United States was very real. During World War II, men and women from the Coast Guard trained in St. Augustine and used the lighthouse as a lookout post for enemy ships and submarines that frequented the coastline.

As was the case with many lighthouses around the country, St. Augustine became automated in 1955. This began the decline of the lighthouse complex. James L. Pippen, who was the last keeper, retired and a lamplighter was assigned. The lamplighter lived off-site and checked on the automatic systems. This position ended in 1989.

St. Augustine

St. Augustine. This First-order Fresnel lens is the largest of all Fresnel lenses. They are most often used in coastal lights.

St. Augustine. To reach the lantern room, visitors climb the 219-step staircase.

St. Augustine. Anastasia Lighthouse postcard. *Authors' collection*

In 1969, the boarded-up keeper's house was declared surplus and put up for sale. Sadly, on July 28, 1970, the keeper's quarters were destroyed by arson. St. John's County bought this property in 1971, including the remains of the keeper's home. It took until 1980 for an organization step-up to care for the property and renovate its buildings. The Junior League of St. Augustine championed the St. Augustine Light and was responsible for getting it listed on the National Register of Historic Places (1981). In 1982, they signed a ninety-nine-year lease with the county. Over the course of fourteen years, they proceeded to raise $1.2 million dollars to complete the project. Thanks to their persistent effort, St. Augustine is one of the most historically accurate aids to navigation in the country. In 1988, the keeper's quarters were turned into a museum, and in 1993 the light was relit. A year later, the tower was restored for climbing and the lighthouse and museum were opened full time to the public. On July 20, 2002, the lighthouse tower was deeded to the St. Augustine Lighthouse and Museum, Inc., which still manages it today.

In 2015, the lighthouse was refurbished in time for the 450th birthday of the city of St. Augustine. The museum, the keeper's quarters, and farm are open to the public. Climbing to the top of the tower is also allowed. In 2018, the St. Augustine Lighthouse and Maritime Museum achieved accreditation by the American Alliance of Museums, the highest national recognition afforded to the nation's museums. Today it stands as one of the most beautiful lighthouse complexes in the South. They host school and archeological maritime programs as well.

St. Augustine

St. Augustine. A quarter-horsepower electric motor is used to turn the First-order Fresnel lens and create its distinctive flashing-light pattern.

St. Augustine. Keeper's quarters and lighthouse in 1824. *Courtesy of the US Coast Guard*

St. Augustine. Historical photo of visitors in their Sunday best. *Courtesy of the US Coast Guard*

Ponce Inlet. This is one of the best restorations of a lighthouse complex in America. *Courtesy of J. Hyland*

PONCE DE LEON INLET (MOSQUITO INLET)
(1835, 1887)

The Ponce de Leon Inlet Lighthouse is located at the southern end of the barrier island adjacent to Daytona Beach. Ponce Inlet was originally called Mosquito Inlet in the 1800s, and the light was also called by that name.

In 1830, ship captains and local farmers petitioned Congress for a lighthouse. It was originally build in 1835 as a 45-foot structure on the south side of the inlet. A terrible storm eroded the base and the lighthouse became weakened. The Seminole Indian War made it impossible to reach the lighthouse for necessary repairs, and so it collapsed in a huge storm before it was ever commissioned. The keeper's quarters were swept away as well.

The Ponce de Leon Inlet Lighthouse, which is 175 feet tall, is the tallest lighthouse in Florida and the second tallest on the East Coast; Cape Hatteras Lighthouse, at 193 feet, is the tallest light on the East Coast and in the country. In 1887, on the northern side of the inlet, the tower was built of red bricks, made in Baltimore. The brick foundation is 45 feet wide and 12 feet deep. The diameter of the tower is 32 feet wide and tapers up to the lantern room. George Meade, the notable lighthouse designer and Civil War general, established a First-order Fresnel lens in the lantern room. A five-wick kerosene lamp first powered it. Oil for the remote lighthouse was transported in small boats and carried by hand to the lantern room, 203 steps from the ground.

Island living was harsh for the lighthouse keepers and their families. Once a year, the government would bring all the supplies needed, including 500 gallons of kerosene. Winters were difficult, with frequent nor'easters. Spring and summer was grueling, with swarms of pesky mosquitos that lived on the island and in nearby swamps. The Spanish had named this area "Los Mosquitos" because of the insects living there. Over time, the name of Mosquito County was changed to Orange County. The Mosquito River in Volusia

Ponce Inlet. These granite steps lead into the base, and a spiral staircase of 203 steps leads to the lantern room.

East Coast Lights: Amelia Island to Cape Florida

Ponce Inlet. This First-order Fresnel lens used to light the Cape Canaveral Lighthouse.

Left: Ponce Inlet. Dedicated volunteers help make this site a "must see" on Florida's East Coast.

Below: Ponce Inlet. Note the windmill in this ca. 1910 photo. It may have been used to operate the well. *Courtesy of the US Coast Guard*

County was renamed Halifax River, and the Mosquito Inlet was renamed Ponce de Leon Inlet in 1926, after the explorer who discovered Florida.

In 1970, the lighthouse was replaced with a metal tower at the Smyrna Dunes Coast Guard Station. The lighthouse was dormant for two years until it was deeded to the citizens of Ponce Inlet in 1972. It was recommissioned or relit in 1983, when a condominium complex in New Smyrna Beach blocked the metal tower light.

In 2004, the museum staff completed the restoration of the rotating Third-order Fresnel lens (1933), and it was reinstalled in the tower. The Ponce de Leon Inlet Lighthouse Preservation Association maintains the Ponce Inlet Lighthouse. The grounds are open to the public for a fee. Tower climbs offer an outstanding view of the ocean and Halifax River. Visitors can spend the day browsing their museum, which contains the First-order Fresnel lens from Cape Canaveral Lighthouse. A Third-order Fresnel lens that used to light Ponce Inlet can also be seen, along with the keeper's quarters and several outbuildings. The gift shop, coupled with the beautiful grounds, makes this complex one of the finest in Florida.

Looking down the stairwell of the Ponce Inlet Lighthouse.

Ponce Inlet. "Beauty of Daytona Beach" historical postcard. *Authors' collection*

LIGHTSHIPS OF FLORIDA (1825–1954)

Lightships were used in America for 160 years. From 1825 to 1985, they marked dangerous moving sandbars, shoals, low water, harbor entrances, river mouths, or places where lighthouses could not be built. A total of 120 stations were established on America's coastlines and the Great Lakes.

In Florida, there were six locations where lightships were assigned. The first lightship ("AA") was assigned in 1825 to Carysfort Reef, which was located in the Florida Straits off Key Largo. It was moored close to the site of the present Carysfort Reef Light. The second lightship ("BB") was assigned to Carysfort Reef in 1841, until it was decommissioned in 1852 when a reef light was constructed. The third lightship location, assigned in 1838, was Northwest Passage (Key West). It was located about 7 miles north and west of Key West. It was replaced by the Northwest Passage Lighthouse in 1854. In 1846, the fourth lightship location was Sand Key, located 7 miles southwest from Key West. It was replaced by the Sand Key Lighthouse in 1853. The fifth lightship was positioned in 1857 at Dames Point in the St. Johns River. It was replaced by the Dames Point Lighthouse in 1863. The last Florida lightship (*LV-84*) was positioned about 5 miles offshore at the entrance to the St. Johns River. It served mariners from 1929 to 1954, when it was replaced by the Mayport Lighthouse.

East Coast Lights: Amelia Island to Cape Florida

Cape Canaveral. A sunny morning rocket launch at Cape Canaveral. *Courtesy of the Cape Canaveral Lighthouse Society*

CAPE CANAVERAL
(1848, 1868)

Cape Canaveral is most known for the aerospace industry. Located 50 miles south of Daytona Beach and due east of Titusville and the Kennedy Space Center, the Cape Canaveral Lighthouse sits on a desolate barrier island where rocket research and the race to outer space was born. The historic grounds of Cape Kennedy Air Force Station are a beautiful location for this lighthouse. It majestically overlooks the Atlantic Ocean to the east and the Banana River to the west.

Ponce de León, the famous Spanish explorer, first spotted this spit of land in 1513 as he sailed from Puerto Rico north along the coast in search of gold. The treacherous currents off the coast of this island led him to name this Cabo de las Corrientes, which means Cape of the Currents. Others named it Canaberal, which means "place of reeds or cane."

Hundreds of years passed, and hundreds of ships sank off the shore. The numerous shoals caused local builders to erect a 60-foot tower in 1848 to warn ships. However, as they sailed closer to the shore to find land, they were shipwrecked. Prior to the Civil War, engineers started to build a 145-foot tower to replace this one, using materials from the original light. Some accounts reveal that the foundation of the present-day lighthouse was constructed of bricks from the first lighthouse. As the first tower was disassembled, bricks were hauled over by mules along train rails. This took about ten months. The work was stopped because of the Civil War and the Confederate secretary of the navy shut off all lighthouses on the East Coast.

Captain Burnham, the first keeper (appointed in 1853), buried the lamp and the clock works in his orange grove near the Banana River, where he supported his family during the war as a farmer. In 1865, at the end of the Civil War, he moved the lamp back to the tower, and construction on the second tower was resumed.

In 1867, a steam engine was used at the site to dewater it so that construction of the new lighthouse could continue. The lighthouse was completed on May 8, 1868. This cast-iron-plated, 145-foot tower is lined with brick and contains black-and-white-striped day markings, similar to the Bodie Island Lighthouse in the Outer Banks of North Carolina. The light can be seen 18 miles out to sea.

Horrendous currents and waves caused concern to the lighthouse keepers, as the ocean made its way to the tower. Jetties were built in an effort to protect Cape Canaveral Light from being washed away. Eventually, the tower was dismantled and moved a mile inland. It was rebuilt at its current site, and a new lens was lit

Cape Canaveral. This early photo shows the keeper's quarters, which are no longer there. *Courtesy of the Cape Canaveral Lighthouse Society*

in July 1894. One interesting feature is the Roman numerals on the stairs inside the tower. Some believe the workers placed these there as an aid to reassemble the lighthouse at this site. There are 179 steps from the ground to the lantern room. Another unique feature is the entrance door on the third level of the tower, which may have been installed to protect the tower from the sea or flooding. There was an outdoor staircase to the third floor, which remained in use until another door was added at the ground level in the 1930s.

During World War II, this area was noted for German subs sinking Allied ships. Spotters manned the tower at night to alert the Coast Guard of submarine activity. In all, twenty-four ships were sunk off the coast, and the Coast Guard rescued over five hundred seamen. Authorities dimmed the light at this location until the war was over. It has remained lit ever since.

Aerial view. This is a 1960s photo of the lighthouse complex. *Courtesy of the US Lighthouse Board–1900*

The Coast Guard assumed responsibility for it in 1939. The area around the lighthouse was incorporated into the Cape Canaveral Air Force Station after World War II. After the Kennedy assassination in 1963, President Lyndon Baines Johnson named this area "Cape Kennedy," after the late president. Later, federal authorities renamed this island "Canaveral" and reserved "Kennedy" for the space program area. In 2000, stewardship was transferred to the 45th Space Wing, Patrick Air Force Base.

Access to tour the lighthouse is limited. Visitors can be admitted only through a Florida Lighthouse Association tour or military clearance. There is a small museum near the entrance gate of the military compound, which also houses a small gift shop. Lighthouse memorabilia can also be purchased in the shop in the base of the lighthouse. The Cape Canaveral Lighthouse Foundation, which co-manages it with the 45th Space Wing of the US Air Force, is working to preserve the lighthouse and increase its access to the public. In 2018, it celebrated its 150th anniversary!

Jupiter Inlet. This light was designed by General George Meade. *Courtesy of J. Hyland*

JUPITER INLET
(1860)

Jupiter Inlet Lighthouse is located in Jupiter on the north side of Jupiter Inlet, between the Cape Canaveral and Hillsboro Inlet lighthouses. Built in 1860, it was first lit on July 10 of that year. It was designed by the famous George Meade, a career US Army officer and civil engineer who was responsible for the design and construction of many coastal lighthouses.

Visitors to this historic landmark will find it positioned at the junction of Jupiter Inlet and the Indian River. It sits on a mound that was regularly used by ancient Indians as a meeting place. Historians originally thought that this mound was a burial site, but later learned that it is merely a parabola-shaped sand dune. Work began on top of the 40-foot mound, and 500 tons of construction materials had to be brought through the Indian River Inlet. The Third Seminole War (1855–1858) interrupted the work and led the workers to build the keeper's quarters with coquina wall to protect themselves from the Indian siege. The lighthouse is constructed of brick and double masonry walls and stands 156 feet tall. At ground level, the walls are 31.5 inches (eight bricks) thick and taper to 18 inches (three bricks) thick just below the lantern. The circumference is 65 feet at the base and gradually decreases to 43 feet at the top.

Our favorite companion, Bodie, often accompanied us to visit Florida's lighthouses.

East Coast Lights: Amelia Island to Cape Florida

Jupiter Inlet. The lighthouse is a short walk from the visitors center. *Courtesy of J. Hyland*

Jupiter Inlet

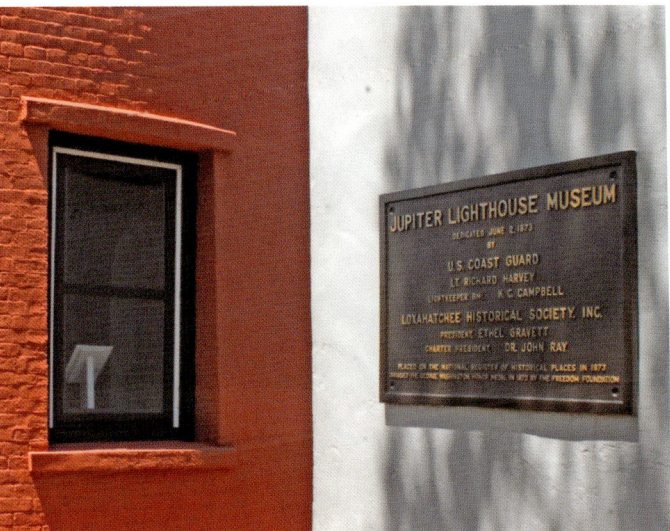

Top: Fresnel lens. A 1,000-watt bulb illuminates this First-order Fresnel lens.

Right: On June 2, 1973, the lighthouse was placed on the National Register of Historic Places and awarded the George Washington Honor Medal.

Staircase. There are 112 steps to reach the top, offering visitors a beautiful view of Jupiter Inlet and the grounds.

Jupiter Inlet. The tower walls are 31.5 inches thick at the base and taper to 18 inches at the top.

Jupiter is distinguished by its red color and black lantern. These colors are known as "day markings," which allow ships and boats to determine their location during the day. There are 112 cast-iron stairs ascending to the lantern room, which contains a First-order Fresnel lens. This lens was manufactured in Paris and is believed to be the oldest existing First-order lens in Florida. A 1,000-watt, quartz-iodine bulb, manufactured by General Electric, powers its light. Its beam can be seen between 17 and 24 miles out to sea.

In 1928 it was electrified. It uses a one-third horsepower motor to turn the lens carriage. On July 1, 1939, all lighthouses in America became the responsibility of the Coast Guard. Like many lighthouses around the country, a photovoltaic panel, combined with a battery, now powers Jupiter. The light comes on and off automatically by a photosensor. With this present-day automation in place, there is no need for a lighthouse keeper.

The military acknowledged this as a key strategic military site. In 1939, the Naval Radio Station constructed barracks for naval personnel and their families. In July 1940, the US Navy's Radio Detection Finding Station, known as "Station J," came online. This secret installation intercepted German U-boat radio messages, warned Allied ships, and pinpointed names and locations of enemy submarines. In May 1943, thirty German submarines were destroyed, and in June another thirty-seven. Most had been located by the men of Station J.

Jupiter Inlet. Historical postcard of Jupiter Inlet. *Authors' collection*

On January 11, 1972, the Loxahatchee River Historical Society (LRHS) was founded to preserve the area's history. It opened the Oil House Museum in June 1973, and on November 15, 1973, the Jupiter Inlet Lighthouse was placed on the National Register of Historic Places.

In 1988, the LRHS opened the Florida History Center and Museum in Burt Reynolds Park, just across the inlet. On December 7, 2006, the history museum and society headquarters moved to Lighthouse Park to become the Jupiter Inlet Lighthouse and Museum. Operations for the lighthouse and history museum are now in one location.

Automated clockworks. These 1860s clockworks are still operating to rotate the Fresnel lens to create a flashing pattern.

The LRHS entered into an agreement with the Coast Guard in 1994 to maintain the lighthouse and conduct regular public tours to the top of the lighthouse. There is a small visitor center and gift shop in the east end of the last remaining building of Station J, once used as living quarters for the military. Throughout this picturesque property are numerous outdoor history exhibits, which describe the Indian cultures that once lived there and the use of the lighthouse and property during the Second Seminole, Civil, and Second World Wars.

Today, the LRHS operates the Jupiter Inlet Lighthouse and Museum and manages the lighthouse climbs during normal business hours, weather permitting.

East Coast Lights: Amelia Island to Cape Florida

Hillsboro Inlet. Located in Pompano Beach, the lighthouse was lit in 1907. *Courtesy of J. Hyland*

HILLSBORO INLET
(1907)

The Hillsboro Inlet Lighthouse is located at Lighthouse Point in Pompano Beach (Broward County), on the northern side of the inlet. It can also be viewed from the south side of the inlet near the Coast Guard Station or on the grounds of the private Hillsboro Beach Club. It was strategically cited here so that ships could sail up and down the coast, always having a lighthouse in view. The first request to Congress was in 1886, and funds were released from 1902 to 1905.

This lighthouse had an interesting birth. A steel company in the Midwest built it in 1904 for the Great St. Louis Exposition. The US government bought the cast-iron tower and its Second-order Fresnel lens and moved it to Florida by barge, down the Mississippi River. They set it up after it arrived in Florida, and it was lighted in 1907. At that time, it was one of only a few new lighthouses of the twentieth century.

Hillsboro is an open-framework design with a solid, two-tone tower in the center, reaching to 137 feet. The open metal framework was ideally suited for the strong Atlantic winds at the shore. The lighthouse is anchored by six huge iron piles. The tower is painted white on the bottom and black on top and is capped with a black lantern. The white color on the bottom was chosen to help it stand out from the trees that surround it on its western side.

Lighthouse keepers used to climb 175 stairs to bring kerosene to light the lamp, until 1932, when oil lamps were changed to electricity. When it was electrified, the candlepower was increased to 550,000, which made it one of the strongest lights on the East Coast. In 1966, a 1,000-watt quartz-iodine bulb was installed, which upgraded the candlepower to two million! Today, its 370,000-candlepower light can be seen 28 miles out to sea, as it beams a white flash every twenty seconds.

The Hillsboro area also has had a colorful history. During the great hurricane of 1926, over 600 feet of land and shore between the lighthouse and the ocean was washed away by the 132-mile-per-hour winds, exposing the foundation. To protect the foundation from future storms, a 260-foot stone breakwater was built in 1930.

During Prohibition, lighthouse keeper Thomas Knight's brother built a restaurant on an island west of the inlet. Much of the illegal booze aboard the rumrunner boats that entered the inlet was served at this restaurant, Club Unique. During World War II, Club Unique was rumored to have been a secret meeting place for President Franklin Roosevelt, Prime Minister Winston Churchill, and Prime Minister Anthony Eden. They would often spend time near the lighthouse, as would General Douglas MacArthur and Admiral Chester Nimitz. To this day, the Coast Guard still uses the keepers' cottages for vacations.

East Coast Lights: Amelia Island to Cape Florida

Hillsboro Inlet. To keep the light fueled, the keepers climbed 175 steps. *Courtesy of Smug Mug*

Second-order Fresnel lens. This beehive lens must be cleaned and polished by the lighthouse volunteers. *Courtesy of the US Coast Guard*

Hillsboro Inlet. This 1966 photo illustrates the width of the beach. Beach erosion is a constant threat. *Courtesy of the US Coast Guard*

Hillsboro Inlet. The lighthouse tower, as shown in 1907, stands 137 feet tall. *Courtesy of the US Coast Guard*

The Hillsboro Lighthouse Preservation Society was founded in October 1997 and is responsible for preserving the historic Hillsboro Lighthouse Station. They also preserve the Barefoot Mailmen statue, located on the grounds of the lighthouse. They host tours and have a museum and an online gift shop. They also host a webcam of the inlet on their website.

US LIFE-SAVING SERVICE

Thousands of lives have been saved from ships in distress since America was first settled in the seventeenth century. Some were saved by men in uniform from the US Life-Saving Service, and some by private citizens. The eastern shores of America were sparsely populated in the beginning. Anyone in a shipwreck in those days would be lucky to find help. That is when the US Life-Saving Service was formed. The organization was responsible for building lifesaving stations along the coast and also "houses of refuge."

The service originated in Massachusetts in the 1800s, founded by a group of volunteers. The men came from all occupations, such as fishermen, crabbers, lobster catchers, and others who lived along the coast. They risked their lives saving shipwrecks, often in dangerous conditions of high wind and waves or subzero temperatures. The motto of the Life-Saving Service was "You have to go out, but you don't have to come back."

Early lifesaving stations were manned with rescue equipment such as life cars, life boats / surf boats, and breeches buoys. Lifeboats were large boats that sat deep in the water and were rowed by eight to ten men. They weighed approximately 4,000 pounds and were difficult to launch, especially in places with soft sand. In the early days of rescuing mariners, this was the only technology available. Surf boats were then used, which were much more practical in Atlantic rescues. They were shorter and much lighter, weighing only 1,000 pounds. Both types of boats had self-righting and self-bailing features.

Life cars were made of iron and resembled small submarines. The life car contained a hatch on top that allowed two to four sailors to climb aboard. Two rings at each end of the covered boat allowed it to be pulled ashore by surfmen. This rescue was dangerous, especially during storms. The use of the life car was diminished by the invention of the breeches buoy.

First, the crew would set up rescue equipment at the shore. A Lyle gun was used to shoot a projectile / whip line at the distressed ship. Once the whip line was secured on the ship, it was connected back to shore, which had to be firmly anchored in the sand. After a series of ropes and pulleys were in place, a breeches buoy, which consisted of a cork-filled life preserver attached to a pair of short pants, would be sent to the ship. Each person had to climb into the buoy and be pulled ashore by the main line. Since persons had to be transported to the shore one at a time, the rescue process took hours.

Surfmen at the station were required to take a shift at daily watches. The watches were timed walks that required the men to walk the beaches in opposite directions from the station. The stations were positioned 4–6 miles apart.

US Life-Saving Service

Life-Saving Service—Island Beach, New Jersey. *Courtesy of US Coast Guard*

The surfmen walked 2–3 miles and were greeted by surfmen from the adjacent station. Today in America, about 115 life stations still stand as a monument of a great maritime era. Florida had two fully manned lifesaving stations, located at Santa Rosa Island (near Pensacola) and Jupiter Inlet.

The Life-Saving Service also built houses of refuge to provide shelter and food for shipwrecked mariners. The original houses-of-refuge system had failed in New England because shipwrecked victims also needed surfmen and boats to assist them in reaching the shore. In April 1871, Congress appropriated $200,000 to form the US Life Saving Service. Sumner Kimball, a lawyer from Maine, was appointed to lead the organization. He made sure that all stations were fully staffed and supplied. In 1915, the service became the US Coast Guard. By this time, there were 279 stations around the country, including Alaska.

Florida was the only state where the Life-Saving Service built houses of refuge. Four houses of refuge were built in 1876, one in 1885, four in 1886, and one in 1896, all on the East Coast of Florida. The houses averaged 26 miles apart, some with a lighthouse in between. From north to south, they include

Smith's Creek (Matanzas Inlet)	Gilberts Bar (or St. Lucie Rocks)
Mosquito Lagoon	Cape Malabar
Chester Shoal	Orange Grove
Indian River/Bethel Creek	New River / Fort Lauderdale
Indian River Inlet	Biscayne Bay (Miami Beach)

Life-Saving Service patrolling. *Courtesy of National Archives*

They were built of Florida pine, with the intent to withstand a hurricane. In Florida, houses of refuge were staffed by a full-time keeper and his family. They contained cots, food, water, clothing, and medicine for rescued mariners. The goal was to be able to provide accommodations for up to twenty-five people for ten days. Although there were no crew or surfmen at the houses of refuge, they always had someone there to protect and maintain the house and protect its contents.

Most of these houses were demolished during hurricanes, and Gilbert's Bar House of Refuge is the only one that remains today, located on Hutchinson Island. It was built in 1876 and has weathered many hurricanes. It is now owned by Martin County and is leased to the Martin County Historical Society, which operates it as a museum. It is the oldest surviving building in the county. Visitors can enjoy exhibits of lifesaving equipment that was used in the past, and the original keeper's quarters. On May 3, 1974, it was added to the National Register of Historic Places.

BAREFOOT MAILMEN

There is a statue honoring the Barefoot Mailmen on the grounds of the Hillsboro Lighthouse. The first postal carriers on the US mail route between Palm Beach and Miami delivered the mail barefoot. Between 1885 and 1892, their route began in Palm Beach and Lake Worth in the north and ended in Miami to the south. In those days, there was no road to connect this 68-mile stretch, and so they used boats and walked barefoot to deliver the mail.

The 136-mile route took six days. On Monday morning, the carrier would leave Palm Beach by boat to the south end of Lake Worth Lagoon. After walking over the beach to the Orange Grove House of Refuge (in Delray Beach), he would spend the night. On Tuesday, he would walk the beach to the Ft. Lauderdale House of Refuge and spend the night. He would travel by boat on Wednesday to the New River Inlet and walk the beach to the north end of Biscayne Bay. Finally, he would travel by boat to Miami. On Thursday, he would begin the return trip back to Palm Beach, where he would arrive on Saturday.

These mail carriers had perfected the method of walking long distances barefoot on the sloping sand without getting tired. The "barefoot mailmen" were also called "beach walkers" or

Barefoot Mailman. On March 19, 2012, the Hillsboro Lighthouse Society unveiled this 8-foot statue. *Courtesy of Hillsboro Lighthouse Society*

"beach walkists." The route continued until 1892, when a rock road was built. This is a fascinating but neglected part of Florida's history. It illustrates another important use of the "houses of refuge," which were positioned along the eastern shores of Florida.

Cape Florida. Located in Bill Baggs State Park in Key Biscayne.

CAPE FLORIDA
(1825)

Bill Baggs Cape Florida State Park is the home of this stately coastal light, which is located on the southern end of the exclusive island of Key Biscayne. The white-sand beach and turquoise water surrounding the lighthouse are picturesque and tranquil. However, this area used to be known for Indian attacks, pirates, fires, and hurricanes.

This barrier island's first inhabitants were the Tequesta, a tribe of the Calusa. Ponce de León stopped here in 1513 and called it Santa Maria. The famous pirate Black Cesar terrorized this coast and was hanged in 1718. In May 1822, Congress appropriated nearly $11,000 for the construction of this lighthouse. A contract to build it and two others in Florida was awarded to Samuel B. Strong of Boston in July 1824. Strong set sail with his crew, his plans, and materials. Sadly, his ship sank and there were no survivors.

Noah Humphries took over the project, and the lighthouse was officially operational on December 17, 1825. This 65-foot coastal light is painted white and has a beautiful black lantern. The plans were to build the base of brick, 5 feet thick, and to taper the structure to 2 feet thick at the top. Unfortunately, the builder scrimped on the materials, and the walls were hollow and frail.

The year 1835 was a difficult time in the history of this lighthouse; it and the keeper's home were severely damaged during a hurricane. During the Second Seminole War, which started in 1835, the Seminole attacked the lighthouse. It was badly damaged by shelling, and the Indians set fire to the wooden door, which resulted in the interior oil tank catching fire. John Thompson, the assistant lighthouse keeper, along with a helper named Henry, climbed the tower with their muskets and a keg of gunpowder. They were forced outside by the fire, onto the platform, where Henry was shot and killed. Thompson decided to attempt suicide by throwing the gunpowder into the fire, which was contained in the lighthouse. His suicide attempt was unsuccessful, but the explosion was heard over 12 miles away by a US Navy ship. This ship ended up rescuing the battered keeper.

The light was extinguished between 1836 to 1846. A rebuild of the lighthouse and keeper's home began in 1846, using materials from the first lighthouse along with bricks from Massachusetts. The lighthouse was relit in April 1847, using seventeen Argand lanterns with 21-inch reflectors.

East Coast Lights: Amelia Island to Cape Florida

Lost but not forgotten. The tower was taken out of service in 1878 and was not refurbished until 1996.

Cape Florida. The tower was raised from 65 to 95 feet in 1855. *Courtesy of J. Hyland*

Cape Florida. Healthy sand dunes protect the Cape Florida Lighthouse from erosion.

Keeper's quarters. The visitors center and gift shop are housed in the former keeper's quarters. *Courtesy of J. Hyland*

In 1855, Cape Florida was raised from 65 to 95 feet to improve its reach out beyond the shoals. Still, there were many shipwrecks on the reefs in this area. During this year, a Second-order Fresnel lens, transported down to the site by George Meade, of the US Army Corps of Topographical Engineers, replaced the lamp. This more powerful light was relit in March 1856. In 1878, the lighthouse was taken out of service, and a new screw-pile, iron lighthouse was built on Fowey Rocks, 7 miles southeast of Key Biscayne. After the lighthouse was taken out of service, it quickly went into disrepair.

In 1966, Florida bought 406 acres on the southern tip of Key Biscayne and made it a state recreation area. The acreage was named after Bill Baggs, a Miami newspaper editor who worked to promote this site as a park and recreation area. Due to the generosity of the Dade County Heritage Trust, Florida state matching funds were acquired to add to monies raised by private donors. Together, $1.5 million was collected to refurbish and maintain Cape Florida. In 1968, the US Army Corps of Engineers placed large rocks in front of the lighthouse to protect it from erosion.

Summer storm. An 1870 photo illustrates an approaching storm. *Courtesy of the US Coast Guard*

One hundred years after the light was darkened, the US Coast Guard installed a light on July 4, 1978, to serve as an aid to navigation once again. The tower underwent a million-dollar restoration in 1996, and the replicated keeper's cottage and cookhouse serve as an interpretive museum. Rangers give tours of the lighthouse compound. Today Cape Florida offers spectacular views of Miami and Miami Beach, as well as Stiltsville, which is a collection of old fishing shacks built over the reefs. The lighthouse is on the National Register of Historic Places.

CHAPTER 5:
The Florida Keys: Fowey Rocks to Dry Tortugas

The Florida Keys: Fowey Rocks to Dry Tortugas

Henry Flagler was influential in real estate along the East Coast of Florida from St. Augustine to Palm Beach. Flagler made his fortune while working as John D. Rockefeller's partner at Standard Oil Company. After building the giant Ponce de Leon Hotel and the Alcazar Hotel in St. Augustine, Flagler expanded his railroad line to Daytona Beach and eventually Miami. In 1905, he made a bold move to build the overseas highway to Key West. At one time during construction, four thousand men were employed. During the seven-year construction, three hurricanes (1906, 1909, and 1910) threatened to stop the project. The project cost was more than $50 million.

Despite the hardships, the final link of the Florida East Coast (FEC) Railway to Trumbo Point in Key West was completed in 1912. That year, Flagler rode the first train into Key West aboard his private railcar, marking the completion of the railroad's overseas connection to Key West and linking the railway along the entire East Coast of Florida. This new rail line was widely known as the "Eighth Wonder of the World." If it had not been for Flagler, the Keys would not be as developed as they are today.

Over the years, multiple hurricanes destroyed certain sections of the railroad tracks. After the hurricane on September 2, 1935, 40 miles of track were washed out, a train was overturned, four hundred people died, and Long Key was demolished. The Florida East Coast Railway became bankrupt and was unable to rebuild the destroyed sections. The roadbed and remaining bridges were sold to the state of Florida, which used the remaining railroad infrastructure to build the Overseas Highway, which still stands today.

The Florida Keys consists of a delicate string of tropical islands stretching 120 miles off the southern tip of Florida, between the Atlantic Ocean and Gulf of Mexico. The southernmost city of Key West is famous for Duval Street's many bars, Mallory Square's nightly sunset celebration, and the Ernest Hemingway Home and Museum. The beautiful aqua waters of South Florida and the unique wildlife draw millions of visitors to the Keys each year.

To add to the tourism value of the Keys, there is a remote national park, Dry Tortugas, located 70 miles from Key West. Also located in the Keys is Fort Jefferson, which is a historic nineteenth-century fort and part of the Dry Tortugas National Park.

The shifting sands in this region have made boat navigation extremely challenging, which also underscores the need for these lighthouses. Before they were built, ships traveling the north–south route of the Atlantic hugged the coastline of the Keys to avoid the powerful Gulf Stream. Numerous shipwrecks are located here and have added to a rich reef environment. Also, the Florida Reef, the only living barrier reef in North America, lies directly off the southeastern coast of Florida, south of Miami. The wrecks are home to abundant marine life and have made the Keys a popular snorkeling and diving destination. There are ten lighthouses in this region of Florida. Six of them are iron-pile lighthouses, known as reef lights. These were built in the mid-1800s and named after notable shipwrecks. The others are conical brick towers.

Of all the lighthouses in this book, these were the most challenging to photograph, since most are located offshore. Because we do not own a boat or an airplane, arrangements had to be made for the photo shoot. We are fortunate to have very good friends with a private airplane who graciously flew us down to take the pictures seen here. We are eternally grateful to Paul and Marilyn Hollowell, and we dedicate this section of the book to them.

The Florida Keys: Fowey Rocks to Dry Tortugas

Fowey Rocks. The light is a screw-pile tower off the northern end of the Florida Reef.

Fowey Rocks. The light was named after the HMS *Fowey*, which sank in 1748.
Inset: Fowey Rocks. This 1937 photograph shows the dwelling enclosed with circular stairs to the lantern room. *Courtesy of the US Coast Guard*

FOWEY ROCKS
(1878)

Fowey Rocks was named after the HMS *Fowey*, a British warship that sank in 1748. It was commanded by Francis William Drake. It is located at the northern end of the Florida Reef, just off the coast of Miami. It has a screw-pile design, is brown in color, and has an octagonal metal-skeleton frame. The stairs are located in an enclosed cylinder in the center of the metal frame. It was built between 1877 to 1878 and was first lit on June 15, 1878. It stands 125 feet above sea level and its 110 feet tall. It originally housed a First-order Fresnel lens, which is now on display in Yorktown, Virginia, at the US Coast Guard's Aid to Navigation School.

Ships that sailed toward the Port of Miami found that the Fowey Rocks Lighthouse was a more reliable aid to navigation than the Cape Florida Lighthouse, which the Lighthouse Board discontinued in 1875. Fowey Rocks is sometimes called "the Eyes of Miami," since it is the first lighthouse seen as ships sail toward Miami from the south.

The Florida Keys: Fowey Rocks to Dry Tortugas

Keeper's area. The living quarters were located 33 feet above the water level.

CARYSFORT REEF
(1852)

Carysfort Reef is home to Florida's oldest reef lighthouse. It is located 6 miles off Key Largo and is named for the HMS *Carysfort*, which ran aground in 1770. Since then, this dangerous reef has claimed many other shipwrecks. From 1833 to 1841, 324 vessels were recorded as lost on the Florida reefs, and sixty-three of them were lost on Carysfort Reef.

Prior to the construction of this lighthouse, two separate lightships were placed here to warn ships of this dangerous reef. The first lightship was the *Caesar*. It headed to the Keys from New York and was marooned off Key Biscayne during a storm. It was towed to Key West to be fixed before being anchored at Carysfort Reef. After a few years, it was retired due to major dry rot. The *Caesar* was the shortest-lived lightship in the history of the US Lighthouse Service.

The second lightship, the *Florida*, fared much better than its predecessor, but its crew did not do well. John Whalton, the keeper of the lightship *Caesar*, was also the keeper for the *Florida*. When Whalton's family visited on June 26, 1837, Whalton and four crewmen rowed ashore to Key Largo, where the crew had a garden to supplement their rations. Captain Whalton and one of his men were killed by Native Americans, and three others escaped. They were later scalped and left on land. Luckily, Captain Cold, of the schooner *Pee Dee*, and Captain English, from the sloop *Brilliant*, and his crew risked their lives and retrieved the remains. The schooner *Pee Dee* had also provided assistance after the Seminole attacked Cape Florida Lighthouse the previous summer.

After the *Florida* was retired, Winslow Lewis proposed a masonry tower. A screw-pile design, submitted by his nephew I. W. P. Lewis, was selected instead. The wrought-iron tower was forged in Philadelphia and shipped to the Keys. The US Army Corps of Topographical Engineers was responsible for building the tower.

Again, construction of a tower on the coral reef was extremely challenging. The reef had a thin crust with a soft layer of sand beneath. To stabilize the weight of the tower, each foundation pile passed through the center of a large cast-iron disk and then was sunk into the sand until the disks rested on the coral. Unfortunately, the money to build this lighthouse ran out before it was completed. After several men worked on the project, George Meade was brought in to finish it.

It was completed on July 31, 1852, and was built on a framework of nine iron piles. The keeper's house is located at the bottom of the cone, the sides having the same angle as the piles. The floor is 33 feet above the water, and the two-story house is 20 feet high. A 38-foot stairway is enclosed in a cylindrical tower and

Carysfort Reef. This is the oldest Florida Reef light (1852).

reaches from the top of the keeper's house to the lantern. The day markings are dark red, and the piles are black. The doors, windows, and roof of the lantern room are white.

The lighthouse was originally outfitted with eighteen lamps set in 21-inch reflectors, but in 1855 a First-order Fresnel lens replaced the array of lamps at a cost of $22,000. A revolving First-order Fresnel lens was activated in the lantern room on March 17, 1858, when the new lighthouse on Sombrero Key was established. The Carysfort Reef signal changed from a fixed white light to a bright flash every thirty seconds. On April 30, 1893, three red sectors were added to the light to indicate hazardous areas.

By the 1920s, the Lighthouse Service decided to change the light patterns along the Florida reefs so that the number of flashes corresponded to the order in which ships encountered the lights. For example, Hillsboro Lighthouse, the first light along the reefs, exhibited a single flash every ten seconds, while Fowey Rocks, the second light, exhibited two flashes every ten seconds. Carysfort Reef was changed to three flashes every twenty seconds, indicating that it was the third light along the reefs. The lens at Alligator Reef was modified to produce a group of four white flashes every fifteen seconds, and a revolving screen was placed inside the fixed lens at Sombrero Key to produce a group of five white flashes every fifteen seconds.

Carysfort Reef

Tranquil day. An 1892 photograph of a calm Atlantic Ocean. *Courtesy of the US Coast Guard*

Carysfort Reef. In 1858, a First-order lens replaced reflectors.

Since it was difficult to count more than five flashes during a storm, the number was reset at American Shoal. American Shoal Lighthouse produced a white flash every five seconds, while Sand Key, the next light along the reefs, produced a group of two flashes every ten seconds. Rebecca Shoal Lighthouse changed its characteristic pattern to three white flashes every fifteen seconds. Authorities planned on changing the light at Dry Tortugas to show four flashes but decided to retain its white flash every twenty seconds since its illuminating apparatus "had proven so satisfactory."

The last keepers left in 1962 and the US Coast Guard automated the light. They replaced the First-order lens in the lantern room with a fixed Third-order lens. In 1982, the Third-order lens was removed when a modern beacon was placed in the tower.

In the 1990s, there was a plan to convert the lighthouse into a marine research center, but this dream was never realized. In 2014, the Coast Guard deactivated Carysfort Reef Lighthouse after determining that the structure was "unstable and considered unsafe." While this lighthouse remains standing, Carysfort Reef's defining characteristic of three flashes per minute is now displayed from a nearby structure at a height of just 40 feet.

The Florida Keys: Fowey Rocks to Dry Tortugas

Alligator Reef. This reef light was named after the USS *Alligator*.

ALLIGATOR REEF
(1852, 1873)

The Alligator Reef Lighthouse, located southwest of the island of Islamorada in the upper Keys, is directly across from Indian Key. It was named after the USS *Alligator*, which is a navy schooner built in Boston in 1820. This ship was originally used to intercept illegal slave boats from Africa that were headed to America. It was also deployed to the West Indies, where piracy was rampant. The USS *Alligator* escorted several ships up the coast from Cuba to the northern states. It was during one of these voyages that it hit a reef off the coast of Islamorada in November 1821.

In 1852, one of the first attempts to mark this dangerous reef was made by Lieutenant James Totten of the US Army Coast Survey. Under his direction, a 36-foot-high, iron-shaft day marker, topped by a black barrel, was placed on a screw-pile foundation. Five years later, it was replaced by a white, hoop-iron cylinder and a red vane displaying the letter "C." It was one of fifteen day markers erected at various dangerous points.

After several petitions to the US Lighthouse Board were made to have a permanent structure at this site, Congress was petitioned for an iron-skeleton lighthouse for Alligator Reef, the request stating, "The only additional aid to navigation required in this district, and the only first class light-house which it is believed is required on any party of the coast of the United States, is one on or near Alligator Reef." Congress did not appropriate the money since it was preoccupied with the Civil War. However, in 1867, another request was made, and requests were repeated until Congress approved it on July 15, 1870.

To begin construction, $100,000 was appropriated and a staging area for the project was located at Indian Key, 4 miles from the reef. The iron-pile lighthouse was forged by Paulding Kemble of Cold Spring, New York, and transported to Indian Key. The lighthouse would be erected near the northeast end of the reef, 30 yards from the original day marker "C," and about 200 yards from deeper Gulf Stream waters.

Building a lighthouse on the reef was an engineering marvel. According to Kraig Anderson of LighthouseFriends.com, "Nine cast-iron disks were arranged on the coral, eight at the corners of an octagon, having a diameter of fifty feet and one at its center. The foundation piles that would pass through the disks were 26 feet long and 12 inches in diameter. A steam-powered pile driver raised a 2,000-pound 'hammer' eighteen feet in the air before gravity brought it crashing down on the pile. Each blow would drive the pile about an inch further in its ten-foot descent into the coral. Atop the vertical foundation piles, six lengths of piles sloped

The Florida Keys: Fowey Rocks to Dry Tortugas

Alligator Reef. The lighthouse was placed into service on November 25, 1873.

Alligator Reef

upwards to the lantern and watch rooms. Running horizontally and diagonally between the piles, a network of braces held the structures together like the filaments in a spider's web. A one-story square dwelling was built on a platform high above the water to keep it safe from even mountainous seas. A spiral staircase sheathed with iron served as the tower's spine, providing structural support and linking the dwelling to the lantern room, over 136 feet above the water."

Alligator Reef was placed into service on November 25, 1873, after an expenditure of $185,000. Its day markings are white, with a black lantern room. The one-story living quarters are painted white, along with the stairs to the lantern room, which are enclosed in a cylindrical tower, located in the center. A revolving First-order Fresnel lens was installed, and in 1884, mineral-oil lamps replaced lard-oil lamps. An oil room was built, which allowed a year's supply of fuel, or 2,200 gallons, to be stored. The light can be seen 15 nautical miles away and has been automated since June 1963.

Alligator Reef. Each year in September, there is an 8-mile swim to the Alligator Reef Lighthouse. *Courtesy of the US Coast Guard*

All the lighthouses off the Keys have experienced hurricanes, high wind, and torrential storms. Most of these lights are remote, and the lives of keepers were lonely and monotonous. Still, they took great pride in keeping their lighthouses in top-notch shape. To commemorate the Alligator Reef Lighthouse keeper and his assistant for their dangerous and excellent work, this light was one of two lighthouses chosen for oil paintings for the Lighthouse Board's exhibit at the World's Columbian Exposition (1893) in Chicago.

Each year in September, there is an 8-mile swim to the Alligator Reef Lighthouse. Swimmers may participate as an individual or in teams up to four persons. This event raises awareness of this lighthouse and raises money for a local scholarship fund.

The Florida Keys: Fowey Rocks to Dry Tortugas

Sombrero Key. Completed in 1858, the light is visible from the north end of the Seven Mile Bridge.

SOMBRERO KEY
(1858)

Sombrero Key Lighthouse is located 7 miles off the coast of Marathon Key, midway between Key Largo and Key West. The lighthouse is built on what was named "Cayo Sombrero" (Hat Island) by the Spanish. The area was also referred to as Dry Bank, since part of the reef frequently could be seen above the waterline. In 1852, a red-and-white barrel, mounted on a 36-foot iron pole, was placed on the reef as a day beacon. The same year, Congress appropriated $35,000 to start work on the lighthouse.

Two years later, George Meade submitted plans and a budget of over $107,000 to start construction. Meade was a West Point graduate who was the leader of the Union forces and responsible for the defeat of Robert E. Lee's Confederates at Gettysburg. After the war, he worked as a survey engineer. He re-enlisted in the army in 1842 and worked for the Army Corps of Topographical Engineers. In 1848, Meade started to work on lighthouse construction. His name is synonymous with lighthouse construction up and down the East Coast in the 1800s. In Florida, he managed the construction of the Carysfort Reef, Sand Key, and Sombrero Key lighthouses. Sombrero Key was the last of the iron-pile lighthouses to be built by Meade.

Originally, the Sombrero Key Lighthouse was designed as a masonry structure. However, due to the expense of building a submarine masonry foundation, Meade decided to build a skeletal style instead. With a focal plane of 142 feet, Sombrero Key Lighthouse is the tallest of Florida's six reef lights.

The foundation consists of eight iron piles, positioned at the corners of an octagon and driven through cast-iron disks to a 10-foot depth. The foundation is sunk into a formation of staghorn and elkhorn coral. Just as with the Carysfort Reef Lighthouse, there is a ninth pile at the center. To prevent saltwater corrosion, all the steel piles are galvanized.

The iron parts for the lighthouse were manufactured in Philadelphia and shipped to Duck Key, which was the construction headquarters. Work commenced in 1856, but a hurricane hit the area on August 27 and 28, and the temporary platform was ruined. Work began again the following year. There were six sections of pilings, supported by cross braces, from the foundation pilings to the lantern room. A one-story keeper's home, consisting of four rooms, totaled only 38 square feet. It was positioned 40 feet above the water on the platform at the bottom of the second section of pilings. The day markings are brown both for the tower and keeper's home. The keepers accessed the lantern room through an enclosed, central circular stairway with 133 steps. A fixed, First-order Fresnel lens, which was made

Sombrero Key. This 1920 photograph shows a lighthouse tender visiting the light. *Courtesy of the US Coast Guard*

in Paris, was installed and brought the total cost of the project to $153,000.

Manning a reef lighthouse was a daunting task. In fact, during a conference of lighthouse officers in 1926, Secretary of Commerce Herbert Hoover told the press, after hearing that most lighthouse keepers were without radios, "I don't know of any of other class of shut-ins who are more entitled to such aid. The government does not pay them any too well, and the instruments, which they can hardly afford, are in many cases their only means of keeping in touch with the world." A radio was donated shortly thereafter.

Riding out a hurricane was terrifying, even with a radio to receive weather updates. In October 1926, the tenth hurricane of the season developed near Panama and passed over Cuba before running east along the Florida Keys. At Sombrero Key, the keepers estimated the wind velocity at 125 miles per hour. Part of the landing platform was washed away, and the ladders were damaged beyond repair.

In 1960, personnel were pulled from the lighthouse and the light was automated. The First-order Fresnel lens was removed from the lantern room in 1982 and is now on display at the Key West Lighthouse. It was deactivated in 2015.

Sombrero Reef continues to be a popular dive and snorkel site. It is visible from the shore at the north end of the Seven Mile Bridge, by using binoculars. Being an offshore light, it is closed to the public, and the dangerous reef prohibits boats from docking.

Sombrero Key. 1950 photo. *Courtesy of the US Coast Guard*

The Florida Keys: Fowey Rocks to Dry Tortugas

American Shoal. Constructed in 1880, the lighthouse was lit by a First-order Fresnel lens.

American Shoal. This 1910 photograph of the wrought-iron lighthouse shows the keeper's dwelling at the 50-foot level. *Courtesy of the US Coast Guard*

American Shoal. Note the American flag in this 1947 photograph. *Courtesy of the US Coast Guard*

AMERICAN SHOAL
(1880)

Plans to build a series of great offshore lighthouses to mark the dangerous Florida Reefs were made as early as 1851. These towers were all skeleton frames, of iron construction, and were built to resist hurricanes. The American Shoal Lighthouse was built to the same plan as the Fowey Rock Lighthouse (1878), and it has the same dimensions.

Located southeast of the Saddlebunch and Sugarloaf Keys, it is southwest of the Looe Key Marine Sanctuary, which is a coral reef within the Florida Keys National Marine Sanctuary. This marine sanctuary includes the Florida Reef, the only coral barrier reef in North America and the third largest in the world.

American Shoal was made of wrought iron from a factory in Trenton, New Jersey, and took thirteen months to fabricate, ship, and erect on-site. It sits 109 feet above the water. The lighthouse was completed in 1880 at a cost of $94,000. It was first lit on July 15, 1880, and was the final iron screw-pile lighthouse to be built on the Florida reefs.

The keeper's octagonal dwelling is on a platform, which sits 40 feet above the water. The tower framework and dwelling are painted brown, while the enclosed circular stair to the lantern is painted white. A First-order Fresnel lens was installed until it became automated in 1963 and a Fourth-order lens with solar-powered light was installed. The current light is a VRN-25 aerobeacon, which requires very little maintenance.

In 1990, the US Postal Service issued a 25-cent stamp featuring the American Shoal Light. American Shoal was deactivated in 2015. A 30-foot-tall tower, topped with an automated light, was built nearby and took over the function of warning mariners of the submerged dangers in the area.

To see the lighthouse from land, turn south onto Sugarloaf Boulevard from the Overseas Highway at Mile Marker 17. When the road tees after 2.6 miles, turn right and drive 2.5 miles to a small bridge over Sugarloaf Creek, from where you can see the lighthouse on a clear day. The lighthouse is currently owned by the Coast Guard and is closed to the public. To get a close-up view of the tower, a boat or plane ride is necessary. The Florida Keys Lights Foundation offers trips each December. Visit their events page for more information on touring the reef lights.

The Florida Keys: Fowey Rocks to Dry Tortugas

Sand Key. Seventeen pilings form the foundation, which is anchored to the coral reef.

SAND KEY
(1827, 1853)

Sand Key is located next to a channel that leads to Key West, approximately 9 miles from the most artsy town in Florida. This area in known for tropical storms, hurricanes, and constantly shifting sand. Over the course of history, three dwellings, one lighthouse, and numerous wharves, privies, and outbuildings were lost to the power of wind and water. Very often, large amounts of sand were deposited on the submerged reefs at Sand Key, which created a small island. After the United States took possession of Florida in 1821, a wooden daymark was placed on the island to warn mariners of this hidden threat to navigation. On May 18, 1826, Congress appropriated $16,000 to build a lighthouse on Sand Key.

The design of the first lighthouse at Sand Key was similar to that of Cape Florida, Key West, and the Dry Tortugas. It was a 60-foot, conical brick tower with eleven lamps, set in 14-inch reflectors. Its light revolved and produced a flashing signature that differentiated it from the nearby fixed light at Key West. It was completed in 1827.

In 1841 and 1842, hurricanes hit Sand Key and destroyed the keeper's home and damaged the lantern. A seawall was built a year later to protect the lighthouse from storm surges that usually accompanied hurricanes. In 1844, the seawall failed, and the newly built keeper's dwelling was destroyed, along with a large part of the island.

On October 11, 1846, the most destructive hurricane hit Sand Key. The keeper and five visitors sought refuge in the lighthouse since the tower had withstood previous storms. Unfortunately, the seawall proved no match for the hurricane. It swept across the island and washed away the dwelling, the tower, and the island itself. The following morning, there was no trace of the lighthouse, the island, or the inhabitants.

Since the reef continued to cause problems for vessels in the area, the *Honey*, a 140-ton ship, was recommissioned as a lightship and sent there. On March 3, 1847, Congress allocated $20,000 for a replacement to Sand Key Lighthouse. An additional $39,970 was added to the budget in 1848. In the meantime, more than eight vessels ran aground on the reef, and all their cargo was destroyed. The urgency to complete the new lighthouse to avoid any more shipwrecks in this area was paramount. Sadly, work was delayed because the control of all US lighthouses was transferred from Stephen Pleasanton, the fifth auditor of the Treasury, to the US Lighthouse Board.

Given the history of Sand Key, the Lighthouse Board chose a screw-pile design. John F. Riley Ironworks in Charleston fabricated the body of the tower, while J. V. Merrick and Son made the lantern room. Seventeen pilings formed the foundation. They were arranged in four-by-four grid around a central pile. Ten-foot borings

SAND KEY IS FOR THE BIRDS

During the time between hurricanes, sand built up around the lighthouse and thousands of terns congregated on Sand Key to nest. Tern eggs, which are extremely tasty, were collected by the lighthouse keepers and delivered to their friends on Key West. Keeper Charles G. Johnson, stationed at the lighthouse in 1902, reported to William Dutcher, the chairman of the American Ornithological Unit, that "nine to twelve thousand birds used to nest on Sand Key, but so many eggs were taken only two to 300 young ones hatched." On neighboring islands, birds were being killed by plume hunters who were looking for fancy feathers to adorn ladies' hats. Dutcher was concerned by the destruction of the bird population and formed a Bird Protection Committee. He hired bird wardens to patrol the islands. Keeper Johnson was one of the wardens, ensuring that Sand Key would be a safe haven for the terns.

anchored the pilings to the coral reef. However, construction was halted again because the funds ran out. An additional $44,000 was appropriated in August 1852, and George Meade was appointed to finish the construction; he had just managed the construction of Carysfort Reef Lighthouse. Construction resumed in January 1853, and the lighthouse was completed and lit on July 20, 1853.

Sand Key Lighthouse is shaped like a pyramid and divided into six horizontal sections. A series of cast-iron sockets at the juncture of each section, united by a system of horizontal tension and diagonal braces, compose this 132-foot-tall structure. Over 450 tons of iron was used in the construction. Within the second horizontal section above the water, a 38-square-foot dwelling consists of nine 12-square-foot rooms. One room contains a 5,000-gallon tank to hold rainwater collected from the roof, and a 1,000-gallon tank for oil. From the dwelling's central room, a spiral staircase with 112 steps leads up a cylindrical tube to the lantern room.

A First-order Fresnel lens, the first one in all of Florida, was placed in the lantern room. It was made in Paris and produces a signal that consists of a repeated cycle of a fixed white light for one minute, a partial eclipse of twenty-five seconds, a white flash of ten seconds, and finally another partial eclipse of twenty-five seconds.

Meade added a few personal touches to Sand Key, such as a hydraulic lamp. This lamp required less maintenance and was soon adopted by the Lighthouse Board. He also used diagonal astragals in the lantern room, which became a distinguishing feature in all of his Florida lighthouses. An astragal is an applied molding that is attached to a door's edge. It protects the structure from harsh weather conditions and can also minimize the passage of light.

After the lighthouse was completed, it was tested by the force of two hurricanes in 1856 and 1865. "Twin Hurricanes" then struck in 1870 and 1875. Most of the island was swept away after each storm, but the lighthouse remained. The station's wharf, boathouse, privy, and oil house were also destroyed multiple times. By 1875, the keeper's dwelling suffered so much damage that it had to be replaced.

To mark dangerous water near the lighthouse, red sectors were added in September 1891. The signature of the light was changed to a group of two flashes every ten seconds around 1930, when a system of numerical flashing characteristics was introduced to the reef lights.

In 1941, after the lighthouse came under the control of the US Coast Guard,

Sand Key. An early photograph shows an island with vegetation. *Courtesy of the US Coast Guard*

the light was automated and the keeper's dwelling was closed. The First-order Fresnel lens remained in the tower until 1967, when it was replaced by a Fourth-order lens.

The Fourth-order lens was removed in 1975 and replaced by a 300 mm lamp. Major renovations, which included replacing corroded parts, sandblasting, and painting, began in 1989. One evening in November, the Coast Guard in Key West received a report that the historic lighthouse was on fire. Apparently, the flammable paints caught fire and were fueled by wooden furnishings from the keeper's dwelling. Most of the damage was contained in the core of the lighthouse, but the intense heat caused the spiral staircase and its cylindrical covering to collapse.

After determining that it was necessary to save Sand Key, the Coast Guard began a $500,000 restoration project in 1994. The keeper's dwelling and cylindrical center column were removed. There was no light in the tower from 1989 to 1998. Finally, a solar-powered VRB-25 aerobeacon was placed atop the lighthouse.

The iron structure still stands over the dangerous reef off the coast of Key West. In 2014, the Coast Guard deactivated it after it proved to be unstable and unsafe. While the historic lighthouse remains standing, Sand Key's defining characteristic of two flashes every fifteen seconds is now displayed from a nearby structure at a height of just 40 feet.

The Florida Keys: Fowey Rocks to Dry Tortugas

Key West. The second lighthouse in Key West was lit on January 15, 1848.

KEY WEST
(1826, 1848)

The town of Key West has always been a strategic point for shipping and trade between the Gulf of Mexico and the Atlantic. It was also a launching point for trade with Cuba and other countries in Latin America and South America. When Spain finally relinquished control of Florida to the United States in 1821, John W. Simonton purchased Key West from a Spaniard for $2,000. Soon, the US government realized the commercial significance of the area.

In 1822, Commander Matthew C. Perry arrived in Florida to survey its reefs. At a minimum, Perry suggested that four lights be built to help mariners avoid the dangerous reefs. These included Cape Florida, Dry Tortugas, Key Largo, and the Sambo Keys. After Congress allocated the funds, Samuel B. Lincoln, who had helped secure the contract for the lighthouses, sailed from Boston for Florida with some of the necessary construction material. Unfortunately, Lincoln, his ship, and all aboard were lost at sea. This shipwreck delayed the construction project, and another schooner was dispatched to Key West.

The *George Stodder* arrived on December 12, and discussions on where to locate the lighthouse at Sambo Keys were initiated. Sambo Keys is an island 7 miles from Key West and was one of many other islands that were frequently inundated. Instead, it was decided to locate the lighthouse at Whitehead's Point, the southernmost point in Key West.

This original Key West Lighthouse was a brick, conical tower measuring 67 feet from its foundation to the base of the lantern. Fifteen lamps, all fueled by whale oil, were officially lit on January 13, 1826, by the keeper, Michael Mabrity. Mabrity's wife, Barbara, was appointed assistant keeper and together they manned the lighthouse. They were also active in the Key West community. Michael, who had served on the town council, died of yellow fever in 1832. His widow, Barbara, was named keeper. She was an amazing woman. As a mother of six children, she not only tended the lighthouse but survived three severe hurricanes (1835, 1841, 1842).

On October 11, 1846, a dangerous hurricane headed toward Key West. The storm surge covered the town in 5 feet of water, and of the 600 island homes, only eight remained after the storm. Fourteen people who sought refuge at the lighthouse died when the tower collapsed. Thankfully, Barbara Mabrity survived the storm, though some of her family died.

After the hurricane, a 30-foot tripod with a signal lantern served as a temporary beacon near the site of the former lighthouse until a replacement tower was built. On March 3, 1847, Congress allocated $12,000 for a new lighthouse.

This First-order lens, which came from Sombrero Key, is on display in the Key West Visitors Center.

Key West. *Courtesy of J. Hyland*

Construction began farther inland in November 1848 and was completed on January 15, 1848, at a cost of $7,247. Although the new tower was only 50 feet tall, it was located on one of Key West's "hills," a parcel of land 14 feet above sea level. A Third-order Fresnel lens, manufactured in Paris, was placed in the Key West Lighthouse in 1858, where it still remains. The lighthouse is white with a black lantern room and is made of brick, granite, and iron.

A keeper's dwelling, made of wood, was completed in 1849, and Mrs. Mabrity resumed her duties. During the Civil War, Key West residents were more sympathetic to the Confederate cause. Mrs. Mabrity, who was vocal about where her loyalties lay, was urged to retire in 1864 for being disloyal. She refused to retire, and so, at the age of eighty-two, she was fired after thirty-eight years of service. She passed away three years later, but her family's legacy at the lighthouse continued.

Her granddaughter, Mary Armanda Fletcher, married John J. Carroll, who was appointed assistant keeper in 1868. In 1870, he was promoted to head keeper. Like her grandmother, Mary served as assistant keeper, from 1876 to March 1889, when her husband died of typhoid. She was promoted to head keeper following his death. Unfortunately, she worked in this capacity for only a few weeks before she also died of typhoid on May 21, 1889. Other keepers related to the Mabritys included their daughter Nicolosa and her husband, Captain Joseph Bethel, who served at the lighthouses on Garden Key and Sombrero Key. Their son, William A. Bethel, replaced his cousin Mary Carroll as keeper and served in this capacity from 1889 to 1908. Upon William's death, his wife, Mary Elizabeth, was promoted from assistant to head keeper and served until 1915, with her son, Merrill, as assistant. In all, the Mabrity family served over eighty-five years at the Key West Lighthouse.

As the town of Key West grew around the lighthouse, it was decided in 1872 to increase the height of the tower by 5 feet. A new lantern room was placed at the peak of the lighthouse. Twenty years later, as trees began to interfere with the light, the superintendent of lighthouses suggested that 25 feet be added to the tower. A balcony was added, and a temporary lens lantern was added in 1893. In 1887, a new and improved keeper's dwelling replaced the original one. This home housed both keepers and their families. Each had their own living quarters, with separate entrances, and they shared a parlor, kitchen, and dining area.

In 1887, the current keepers' dwelling was completed to replace the first quarters at the new site. Designed to house two keepers and their families, the spacious building provided a separate room and entrance for each family, though they did share a common parlor, dining room, and kitchen.

Key West. A view inside the Fresnel lens, which also shows red and clear sectors.

Key West. A 1930s postcard of historic Key West. *Authors' collection*

In 1915, the Key West Lighthouse was converted from incandescent oil vapor to acetylene. This change meant that it did not need a full-time lighthouse keeper and assistant. As technology evolved, the light became automated. Even though these positions were not needed, the lighthouse superintendent and his family moved into the home and remained there until 1939, when the US Coast Guard took over the lighthouse.

In 1966, the Key West Art and Historical Society became responsible for the dwelling. They built a military museum on-site and in 1969 began tours of the tower when the light became deactivated. A renovation project of the tower began in 1987. Hundreds of crumbling bricks were replaced with bricks from Fort Zachary Taylor. The 1887 keeper's quarters was restored next, and the dwelling was opened in 1990 as a lighthouse museum. Military artifacts were removed from the grounds in 1988.

The museum and lighthouse are located at 938 Whitehead Street, across from the Hemingway House. Visitors can climb the ninety-eight stairs to the top for an amazing view and also explore the museum exhibits, which detail life in Key West in the 1800s.

WOMEN KEEPERS OF FLORIDA LIGHTS

Most of the women who were appointed to tend lights were acquainted with lighthouse routines, having learned their duties by helping a father or husband. *Instructions to the Keepers of Lighthouses with the US* from an 1835 Treasury Department document specifically states, "A lighthouse must never be wholly unattended. Where there is a keeper and one or more assistants, either the keeper or one of the assistants must be present. If there is only one keeper, some competent member of his family, or other responsible person, must be at the station in his absence." Teenage children also shared the responsibility for tending the lights, often performing heroic acts in their father's absence. The Lighthouse Service clearly benefited from this extra unpaid labor as families carried on the keeper's duties when he could no longer perform them.

Several brave women were lighthouse keepers in Florida. When Barbara Mabrity's husband died in 1832, she became the lighthouse keeper at the Key West Lighthouse, serving until 1864, when she died at the age of eighty-five. In addition to her lighthouse duties, she raised six children and survived the hurricane of 1846. Although the lighthouse tower collapsed around her in the storm, fourteen people who had taken refuge there were drowned.

Mrs. Mabrity's grandson, William Bethel, became keeper of the light in 1889. When he retired in 1908, his wife, Mary, replaced him as keeper. Her son, Merrill, became her assistant keeper. Mary remained at her post until 1914.

Other notable Florida women keepers included Michaela Ingraham, who replaced her husband, Jeremiah, at the Pensacola Lighthouse from 1840 to 1855. Rebecca Flaherty replaced her husband, John, at Sand Key from 1830 to 1846, and Frances McDonald replaced her husband, Alexander, at St. Johns River from 1871 to 1879. Both Ann Dudley and Sarah Fine replaced their husbands at St. Marks Lighthouse from 1850 to 1854 and 1904 to 1909, respectively.

The Florida Keys: Fowey Rocks to Dry Tortugas

Garden Key. The lighthouse at the top of Ft. Jefferson. *Courtesy of Smug Mug*

GARDEN KEY
(TORTUGAS HARBOR AT FORT JEFFERSON) (1826, 1874)

Garden Key is located in the Dry Tortugas, a small cluster of reefs, islands, and shoals approximately 70 miles from Key West. These islands are located directly on the outer edge of the shipping channel between the Gulf of Mexico and the Atlantic.

Juan Ponce de León was the first to discover these islands, in 1513. He named the area "Las Tortugas," which is Spanish for "the turtles." Although there was an abundance of turtles on these islands, which include Loggerhead Key, Bush Key, Garden Key, Middle Key, Hospital Key, Long Key, and East Key, they were renamed "Dry Tortugas" because of the hot, dry climate and the lack of fresh water.

The British considered building a lighthouse here in 1773, but nothing happened until the United States took ownership of these islands. In 1819, Spain ceded Florida to the United States, and the treaty was officially ratified in 1821. After gaining control of the territory, the federal government dispatched Commander Matthew C. Perry to survey the Florida coastline. He saw the danger posed by the reefs surrounding the Florida Keys and recommended the construction of lighthouses at Cape Florida, Key Largo, Sand Key, and Dry Tortugas. On May 7, 1822, Congress appropriated $8,000 for the construction of Dry Tortugas, but this sum reverted to the treasury. On May 26, 1824, the same amount had to be reappropriated by Congress.

The site selected for the lighthouse was Garden Key, strategically located near the center of the Dry Tortugas so that its light would cover all the islands and mark the harbor just north of the island. The ship that carried the building supplies was lost at sea on its way to Florida, which delayed the start of construction until 1825. In March 1826, the 65-foot-tall, white, conical brick tower was completed. Approximately seventy wooden steps provided access to the black lantern room. The original lighting consisted of twenty-three lamps in 14-inch reflectors. In 1838, there were seventeen lamps in 23-inch reflectors, which improved the signal.

Garden Key was downgraded in 1856 after a taller lighthouse was built on Loggerhead Key. Several months later, the lighthouse keeper and his wife arrived from their home in Baltimore. John R. Flaherty was the first keeper. His wife, Rebecca, despised the heat, boredom, and bugs. After she wrote to the wife of President John Quincy Adams, Flaherty was able to swap posts with the keeper at Sand Key Lighthouse, which was closer to Key West.

Flaherty never took very good care of the lighthouse, and soot built up on the lenses and windows of the lantern room. The inadequate light was an ongoing complaint of the mariners. In 1838, even after the original fifteen lamps were replaced by twenty-three new lamps and reflectors, complaints continued. This lighthouse was important to ships transporting goods from the Gulf of Mexico up the East Coast of the United States. The US military also realized early on that any power, foreign or domestic, that controlled the Dry Tortugas would also control navigation in the Gulf of Mexico.

And so, in 1858, a 150-foot-tall tower was built on Loggerhead Key, 3 miles west of Garden Key. After Loggerhead was completed, Sand Key was downgraded to a Fourth-order harbor light and was renamed "Tortugas Harbor Lighthouse."

A strong hurricane in October 1873 badly damaged the Garden Key Lighthouse. Repairs were made but inspectors still believed that it should be torn down. Congress appropriated $5,000 for a boilerplate iron structure to be built inside the walls of the fort, which had been built in 1846. Construction began on a three-story hexagonal tower, which was first painted dark brown and then black. It was lit on April 5, 1875.

The keeper's home and the soldiers' barracks were destroyed by a fire in 1912. An automated acetylene light was installed in the lighthouse that same year. It was then deactivated in 1921. The remote grouping of islands was designated the Fort Jefferson National Monument by President Roosevelt in 1935 and became the Dry Tortugas National Park in 1992.

Garden Key. A beautiful day overlooking Ft. Jefferson, which was dedicated as a national monument by President Franklin D. Roosevelt in 1935. *Courtesy of J. Hyland*

Garden Key. Ft. Jefferson in 1880, not long after the Civil War. *Courtesy of US Coast Guard*

ACCUSED LINCOLN ASSASSINATION CONSPIRATOR AND FT. JEFFERSON

In 1846, work began on a fort that came to be known as the "Gibraltar of the Gulf." Fort Jefferson, which is America's largest nineteenth-century coastal fort, is located in the lower part of the Florida Keys in the Dry Tortugas. It took sixteen million bricks to build the 45-foot-high walls of the six-sided fort. The walls alone are 8 feet wide. Work on the fort continued for thirty years but was never completed. During the Civil War, when bricks could no longer be obtained from the South, the Union brought bricks from Maine to try to complete the fort. Although the fort was never involved in any battles, it did house over 2,200 prisoners over a ten-year period, with a peak of 900 prisoners in 1864 during the Civil War.

One of the most famous prisoners was Edman Spangler, an employee of the Ford Theater. He was convicted of aiding John Wilkes Booth's flight from the assassination scene of President Abraham Lincoln. Two other men, who were convicted of conspiracy and planning to kidnap President Lincoln, were also sent here. Dr. Samuel A. Mudd, guilty of conspiracy and harboring Booth in his Maryland home, joined the other three in the summer of 1865. Dr. Mudd was held as prisoner from 1865 to 1869.

Yellow fever later struck the prison, and one of the notable prisoners died, along with the fort's doctor. A quarantine station was set up at the nearby Loggerhead Key. In early 1869, the three surviving prisoners related to Lincoln's assassination were pardoned by President Andrew Johnson.

Dr. Richard D. Mudd, the grandson of Samuel A. Mudd, spent most of his adult life waging a campaign to clear his grandfather of complicity in the assassination of President Lincoln. Richard passed away in 2002 at the age of 103, having never fully realized his dream. Dr. Samuel A. Mudd's life was the subject of a 1936 John Ford film, *The Prisoner of Shark Island*, and a 1980 movie, *The Ordeal of Dr. Mudd*, staring Dennis Weaver.

The Florida Keys: Fowey Rocks to Dry Tortugas

The lighthouse on Loggerhead Key was completed in 1858. It is part of the Dry Tortugas National Park.
Courtesy of Smug Mug

DRY TORTUGAS (LOGGERHEAD KEY)
(1826, 1858)

This remote destination is accessible only by private boat, sea plane, or the daily ferry from Key West. Dry Tortugas National Park was created in 1992 and encompasses all seven islands in the Dry Tortugas along with the surrounding coral reefs and shoals. The lighthouse and other Coast Guard buildings on Loggerhead Key were transferred to the National Park Service, though the Coast Guard is still responsible for the light.

Garden Key was one of three lighthouses planned for the Florida Straits, which was a dangerous area for mariners. Construction was completed in 1826 on the 65-foot-tall light. Unfortunately, the iron door of the lighthouse, which housed the lantern, impaired the visibility for ships traveling from the east, and so the door was removed. As more shipwrecks increased in the Garden Key area, it was decided that a more adequate lighthouse was needed. The Dry Tortugas Lighthouse, now known as the Loggerhead Lighthouse, was planned by Congress with an appropriation of $35,000.

Captain Daniel P. Woodbury oversaw its construction while also managing the project at Garden Key's Fort Jefferson, 3 miles away. Loggerhead is a conical, brick tower standing 150 feet tall on this mile-long island. The day markings are white on the lower half of the tower and black on the upper half. A spiral staircase, consisting of 230 granite steps, is enclosed in the center of the tower, leading to the watch room. The tower's brickwork flares to support an exterior walkway around the watch room. A First-order Fresnel lens, made in Paris, was lit on July 1, 1858, and produces a steady white light.

A two-story duplex and a second two-story home were built as housing for the keeper and the assistant. The top floor of the second structure was living space for the second assistant keeper, and the ground floor was used as a shared kitchen. A two-story, freestanding brick oil house and two brick cisterns, which collected the rainwater from the roofs of the two dwellings, were also built.

During the Civil War years, roughly 2,000 people were living at Fort Jefferson on Garden Key, including several officers and their families. Loggerhead Key, as its name implies, was a nesting place for turtles, and men at the fort frequently visited the island to "turn turtle." Innocent turtles would swim up on the beach at night to lay their eggs, only to find themselves rudely inverted and then later hauled off to Garden Key, where they became a valuable source of food. The turtles, which weighed between 200 and 500 pounds, were a common staple for the keepers and their families.

The turtle hunts provided the families living at the fort a chance to socialize

The Florida Keys: Fowey Rocks to Dry Tortugas

Dry Tortugas. Towering 150 feet tall, the lighthouse was electrified in 1931. *Courtesy of Smug Mug*

Dry Tortugas. Living on Loggerhead Key in 1900. *Courtesy of the US Coast Guard*

with those at Dry Tortugas. The wife of an officer at the fort left the following record of one such occasion: "We took three boats, with music for dancing and supper, making a grand frolic of the occasion. After supper, which everyone enjoyed in the lighthouse living room, the ample kitchen was converted into a ballroom, and dancing indulged in until it was time for the turtles to come up."

Both Dry Tortugas and Garden Key lighthouses sustained heavy damage during the hurricane of 1873. On March 3, 1875, Congress appropriated $75,000 for rebuilding the tower at Loggerhead Key, since it was unsafe in high winds. Making the necessary repairs was no small task, since the tower was 150 feet tall and was located in such a remote location. The section of the tower 9 feet below the lantern room and the watch room's walls were entirely rebuilt. Since the construction team did such an excellent job, plans for a replacement tower were dismissed.

The lighthouse keepers shared the island from 1904 until 1939 with the Carnegie Marine Biology Lab. Here, scientists conducted research on the coral reefs and mangroves and took the first-ever underwater photos, both color and black and white. Their research was the first of its kind in the Western Hemisphere. The keepers also shared the island with soldiers during World War II, since this location was strategic to the security of the United States.

In 1931, generators for producing electricity were added in a frame addition to the former oil house. In October 1931, tests were conducted at Fort Jefferson, 3 miles from Loggerhead Key, to measure the effectiveness of three different light sources. An incandescent-oil-vapor lamp, three 250-watt electric bulbs, and one 500-watt electric bulb were compared. The results showed that the single bulb produced a flash of 985,000 candlepower. The three 250-watt bulbs produced a flash of only 404,000 candlepower, while the incandescent-oil-vapor lamp produced only 151,000 candlepower.

After the mercury float was damaged in 1986, and the lens came to a stop, the Coast Guard replaced it with a DCB-24 after they safely disposed of the mercury. In 1995, a VRB-25 replaced the DCB-24. The original lens is now on display at the National Aids to Navigation School in Yorktown, Virginia. Dry Tortugas was the site of the first radio beacon in all of Florida. It transmitted signals during fog and inclement weather. It also sent a signal during clear weather four times a day. The lighthouse was automated in 1987.

After the two-story keeper's home was destroyed by fire in 1945, a new one-story structure was built. Volunteers and rangers for the national park stay in the building that was once used for the kitchen and second assistant. The Coast Guard uses the 1922 home when they are there to service the lighthouse.

GARDEN KEY LIGHTHOUSE FEATURED ON A STAMP

Garden Key Lighthouse was one of five Gulf Coast lighthouses featured on a postage stamp series released by the United States Postal Service in 2009. Known as "hurricane alley," the Gulf Coast weathers many powerful storms each year, including Hurricane Katrina, which devastated the region in 2005. In addition, the land along the coast is swampy and marshy in many places and given to erosion, making it doubly difficult for lighthouses to withstand heavy rains and winds. The five lighthouses featured on the stamps are some of the few that remain standing.

The popular lighthouse series included paintings by artist Howard Koslow of Toms River, New Jersey. Five different stamps each depict a lighthouse. They include Fort Jefferson (also known as Garden Key Lighthouse), Dry Tortugas National Park; Matagorda Island, near Port O'Connor, Texas; Sabine Pass, near Sabine Pass, Louisiana; Biloxi, in Biloxi, Mississippi; and Sand Island, near the entrance to Mobile Bay in Mobile, Alabama.

CHAPTER 6:
West Coast Lights: Cedar Key to Sanibel Island

WEST COAST OF FLORIDA: INVENTORS, TOURISM, COMMERCIAL AIRLINES, AND THE CIRCUS

Many famous Americans settled in western Florida, at least for the winter months. Two of the most famous were Thomas Edison and Henry Ford. In 1885, Edison built a winter home and laboratory in the fishing village of Ft. Myers. His close friend Ford liked the Ft. Myers area and built a home next to Edison's. Edison's first invention, a universal stock ticker, was sold for an amazing sum of $40,000. Edison recorded 1,093 patents, a least one per year from 1868 to 1933. Ford met Edison when Ford was an employee of the Edison Illuminating Company in Detroit. Edison always encouraged Ford, who built prototype cars, including the quadricycle in 1896.

Similar to Henry Flagler influencing the East Coast of Florida, there was another "Henry" who affected the history of the West Coast. Henry B. Plant was an entrepreneur who constructed rail lines from the Tampa Bay area to Punta Gorda. Opening up these towns with the railroad line stimulated tourism. Plant constructed the extravagant Tampa Bay Hotel in 1891, which was designed by J. A. Wood of New York. Mr. and Mrs. Plant visited Europe to procure furnishings, antiques, and artwork. They spent over three million dollars to build and furnish this hotel, which was a great sum back in the late 1890s. Plant died in 1899, and the hotel was sold to the City of Tampa for $125,000. The University of Tampa bought the hotel in 1933, and it is the focal point of their campus. Inside the Tampa Bay Hotel is the Plant Museum, which houses many artifacts from the original hotel.

The West Coast of Florida was also the location for a major technological feat. On January 1, 1914, the first regularly scheduled commercial airline flight took place between Jannus Park in St. Petersburg to Tampa. The pilot was Anthony "Tony" Jannus, who flew a Benoist biplane with one passenger. St. Petersburg's mayor, Abe Phiel, was the passenger, and they carried one bag of mail onboard. Today, a model of the Benoist airplane used by Jannus hangs in the St. Petersburg Museum of History.

Farther down the West Coast, another entrepreneur was shaping the history of Sarasota and Venice. In 1926, John and Mable Ringling constructed Ca d'Zan, a Mediterranean Revival–style mansion that cost $1.5 million, which is equivalent to $40 million today. The Ringlings spent an additional $400,000 on furnishings and fine artwork from Europe. The following year, Ringling decided that Sarasota would become the winter home of his circus. They stayed there from late November to early March. At one time, John Ringling was the fifth-richest man in the country. Unfortunately, his financial mistakes and the Great Depression led to his financial ruin. He passed away in 1936 with just $311 in the bank. He left his mansion and art collection to the State of Florida. In 2000, ownership of the property was transferred to Florida State University. In 1960, the Ringling Circus moved its winter home from Sarasota to Venice, where it remained until 1992.

The shallow waters and shoals from Key West to the deepwater ports of Port Charlotte and Tampa were dangerous for mariners traveling in both directions. Several lighthouses were approved by Congress and built to mark the ports as well as some of the islands where numerous wrecks had occurred. The development of the railroad leading to the ports was instrumental in building the shipping trade, which remains strong today. Phosphorus, which was mined in Florida, was transported by train to ships waiting in Boca Grande. Tampa is a major port for industrial and agricultural products, as well as cruise ships.

West Coast Lights: Cedar Key to Sanibel Island

Cedar Key. George Meade was the architect and builder.

Cedar Key. A 1907 photograph of guests in their Sunday best. *Courtesy of the US Coast Guard*

CEDAR KEY (OR SEAHORSE KEY)
(1854)

Cedar Key is a small island community north of St. Petersburg, between the Suwannee and the Waccassa Rivers. Off the coast of Cedar Key is another small island, Seahorse Key, where this lighthouse stands. A large sand dune, which stands at 52 feet above sea level, was the site chosen for this lighthouse. This elevation is the highest on the West Coast of Florida.

George Meade, the architect for many other lighthouses around the country, was the architect and builder. The Cedar Key Lighthouse is 75 feet tall, was constructed of brick and iron, and has thirty-five steps from the ground to the lantern. It originally had a Fourth-order Fresnel lens and was constructed for only $12,000.

It has been an important aid to navigation since 1854. During the Civil War, the light was extinguished in 1861 by Confederate troops. They dismantled the lens and used the lighthouse station as their headquarters. Union gunboats captured the soldiers, and the lighthouse was used as a prison until the end of the Civil War. Toward the turn of the century, when lumber and fishing in the area had started to decline, large freighters no longer sailed here. This lighthouse was also difficult to see as the trees began to grow around it. It was abandoned in 1915.

A private owner took over the lighthouse and added wings to the lighthouse keeper's wooden structure. The Cedar Keys National Wildlife Refuge, which was created in 1929, uses this light station for wildlife studies. It was originally formed to protect more than 1,000 endangered brown pelicans on the key. Wading shoreline birds were slaughtered by the thousands for their plumage, which was used for ladies' hats. The University of Florida located a marine laboratory at the lighthouse, where it has remained a center for learning about Florida's natural environment.

This lighthouse is accessible only by boat, and visitors may not enter the structure. However, it is open to the public four days a year for tours. Local boat tour companies run shuttles out of Cedar Key on those days, and the Welcome Center has a list of tour dates. Further information on the lighthouse and the history of this area can be seen on the mainland as part of the Cedar Key Museum State Park and the Cedar Key Historical Society Museum.

Cedar Key. The lighthouse tower is 75 feet tall and was completed in 1854. *Courtesy of the US Coast Guard*

Anclote Key. The lighthouse was built as part of the Federal Coastline Defense Program in 1880.

ANCLOTE KEY
(1887)

Anclote Key is a 188-acre island off the coast of Tarpon Springs, northwest of Tampa. The name "Anclote" is a Spanish word meaning "anchor." In the 1880s, it was a popular retreat for dignitaries, tourists, and fishermen. President Grover Cleveland signed an order to have the Anclote Key Lighthouse built in 1887, part of the federal coastline defense program. At the time, it cost the US Lighthouse Service $35,000. This lighthouse guards the mouth of the Anclote River and stands at the southern tip of the island.

The 96-foot-tall skeletal tower is made of cast iron and sits on a concrete base. There are 138 steps from the base to the lantern. On September 15, 1887, the kerosene lamp lit a Third-order revolving Fresnel lens. A cistern and an oil house were also installed around the same time. There were two families who lived on the island and tended to the lighthouse. One keeper raised pigs, which had free roam of the island. Another keeper purchased a canon for self-defense during the Spanish-American War.

Anclote Key. A third-order lens sits on top of the 87-foot cast-iron tower.

The light was automated in 1952. After the light was deactivated in 1985, arsonists burned the outbuildings to the ground. The iron tower fell victim to the elements and became severely rusted. A concerned group of citizens formed the "Relight the Light Committee" and were able to have this lighthouse enlisted on the National Register of Historic Places. It is now owned by the State of Florida and is part of the Anclote Key Preserve State Park. Funds were allocated to refurbish the lighthouse, and it was relit in 2003, using a reproduction Fourth-order Fresnel lens.

This lighthouse contributed to the growth of Tarpon Springs, where it has been the guiding light for many fishermen and sponge divers. Tarpon Springs became incorporated as a city in 1887 and is a thriving town and fishing port today. Prior to the late 1800s, nearly all the sponges in the United States came from the Bahamas or Key West. Before the addition of the lighthouse, mariners from the Apalachicola area, who had been harvesting sponges west of Anclote Key, would travel all the way to the Keys. Now with this lighthouse, boats would make their way to safe harbor in Tarpon Springs. The Tarpon Springs Sponge Exchange became the largest sponge market in the country between 1907 and 1972. Many Greek immigrants began to settle here, and today, Tarpon Springs is still known for its sponges and large Greek settlement.

Anclote Key. This lighthouse contributed to the growth of Tarpon Springs, where it has been a guiding light to sponge divers. *Courtesy of the US Coast Guard, 1913*

West Coast Lights: Cedar Key to Sanibel Island

Egmont Key. Located on a 398-acre island, Egmont was discovered by Spanish explorers in the 1500s.

EGMONT KEY
(1848, 1858)

The Egmont Key Lighthouse is located south of St. Petersburg and west of Tampa Bay in the Gulf of Mexico. It is situated at the northern end of Egmont Key, a historical 398-acre island, positioned at the mouth of the shipping channel. The island, which is 1.6 miles long and a half mile wide, was discovered in the 1500s by Spanish explorers and had a rich history before the lighthouse was constructed in 1848.

Tampa became an important shipping port many years after Spain seceded Florida to the United States back in 1821. Captain Lawrence Rousseau surveyed aids to navigation in the Gulf of Mexico and recommended that a lighthouse be positioned at Egmont Key. After Congress appropriated $7,580, a lighthouse and a keeper's house was built on the island, and the light was lit in May 1848. At that time, it was the only lighthouse between St. Marks and Key West. A hurricane struck the island on September 25, 1848, and damaged both the tower and the lighthouse keeper's house. Several repairs later, a new lighthouse was built in 1858 at a cost of $16,000. It remains standing today and has withstood many severe hurricanes and storms.

Spiral stairs. The tower is 76 feet tall and has ninety-nine steps to the lantern room.

The white tower was 81 feet tall when it was originally built, and 76 feet tall after it was modified in the 1940s. It is made of brick, concrete, and iron and has ninety-nine steps to the lantern room. It originally contained a Third-order fixed Fresnel lens, but today it is an active aid to navigation, with an electric rotating beacon, flashing white every fifteen seconds.

Egmont Key. A 1910 photo shows docks and the keeper's quarters. *Courtesy of the US Coast Guard*

The Civil War adversely affected most of the lighthouses in Florida, and Egmont Key was no exception. George Rikard, the keeper at the time of the Civil War, removed the lens and most of the supplies to keep them out of the hands of Union troops. They were stored in Tampa for safekeeping. In July 1861, Union forces occupied the island and set up a base of operations for the East Gulf Blockading Squadron. The lighthouse was relit in June 1866.

A buoy depot was built here in 1872. By 1889, all the buoys used between Key West in St. Marks were repaired, serviced, and painted at this depot. Between 1898 in 1923, the lighthouse keepers shared the island with Fort Dade, which was one of the Army's important coastal defense installations on the Gulf.

This fort dates back to 1907 and includes over seventy buildings. When one travels to the island for the lighthouse tour, visitors can still see the ruins of Fort Dade, which had electric and telephone service. The small city included a school, post office, theater, hospital, officers' quarters, barracks, morgue, mess hall, storehouse for ammunition, fire station, bakery, and carpenter and blacksmith shops. The eastern part of the island, which is a shorebird refuge maintained by the US Fish and Wildlife Refuge, is closed to the public. At the north and south ends of the island, tourists can view the bunkers that were erected to protect the island during the Spanish-American War. The island was also used to quarantine American soldiers who were returning from Cuba.

During World War I, Coastal Artillery units of the National Guard used Fort Dade as a training center. In 1921, by which time all elaborate coastal defense installations were considered obsolete, the US government deactivated the fort. The military began to use Egmont Key again during World War II. A harbor entrance patrol station and an ammunition storage facility for vessels entering Tampa Bay were placed on the island. They also used the island for amphibious warfare and aerial gun exercises. After World War II, the island was abandoned except for the

Coast Guard, which tended the lighthouse. In 1974, it became a National Wildlife Preserve, and it was added to the National Register of Historic Places in 1978.

Egmont Channel, which is Tampa Bay's main shipping channel, serves several thousand ships a year. The southern end of the island has housing quarters for ship pilots, who meet large tankers and cruise ships and pilot them into the harbor. The Federal Aviation Administration also maintains a radio beacon that guides commercial air traffic into the Tampa Bay airports.

There are boat tour companies throughout Tampa Bay and at Fort Desoto Park to take visitors to the island. The beaches are basically deserted, but visitors may share the island with a colony of gopher turtles, lizards, rattlesnakes, and lots of poison ivy and mosquitoes. Water and restroom facilities are very limited, so plan ahead.

Lighthouse and fort. Ft. Dade was built in 1907 and included a school, post office, theater, hospital, bakery, and fire station.

West Coast Lights: Cedar Key to Sanibel Island

Boca Grande Rear Range. Located a mile north of Boca Grande Lighthouse, it was lit in 1932.

BOCA GRANDE REAR RANGE
(1932)

This lighthouse was constructed by the Phoenix Iron Company in Trenton, New Jersey. It was built in 1927 and was lit in 1932. It is an iron skeletal tower that stands 106 feet tall. Its day markings are white, and it contains an enclosed center staircase in a cylinder.

This is one of the few lighthouses that has had active service in two states. Originally built in 1881, it was located north of Lewes, Delaware. It was known as the Delaware Breakwater Rear Range Lighthouse, but the locals knew it as the Green Hill Lighthouse. Because of shoreline changes, it was discontinued in 1918. The clockworks and lens were shipped to the West Coast of Florida. The remainder of the parts were shipped by railroad to Miami in 1921, when funding became available. Because funding was again delayed, the US Lighthouse Service did not reassemble the lighthouse until 1927.

Boca Grande Rear Range. The lighthouse was decommissioned in 2000, fell into disrepair, and was refurbished by the Barrier Island Parks Society in 2017.

West Coast Lights: Cedar Key to Sanibel Island

Boca Grande Rear Range. This light had active service in Lewes, Delaware, before being moved to Florida in 1932.

Boca Grande Rear Range

It is located approximately a mile north of the Boca Grande Lighthouse. It was never manned, but it was maintained by the keepers of the Boca Grande Lighthouse. It was an important part of the commercial shipping history in the late twentieth century in Charlotte Harbor. The Boca Grande navigation channel was extremely dangerous, and this tower helped guide ships from around the world into safe harbor.

In 1998, Florida Power and Light was the sole commercial user of this light. They announced that by 2001, they would no longer be receiving shipments here, and the light would not be necessary. The US Coast Guard announced in August 1999 that it would be transferred to the General Services Administration and would be disposed of. This skeletal lighthouse remains an aid to navigation today. Recently, the lighthouse was completely refurbished with the help of the Barrier Island Parks Society. Also, tours are available one day a month to climb the tower.

Boca Grande Rear Range. The lighthouse is open one day a month for visitors to climb the 134 steps to the lantern room.

Boca Grande Rear Range. A photograph before the renovations by the Barrier Island Parks Society.

Boca Grande. The lighthouse was lit on December 31, 1890, and stands 44 feet tall.

Boca Grande. An additional wood-frame structure was built for the assistant keeper.

PORT BOCA GRANDE
(GASPARILLA ISLAND) (1890)

Boca Grande. A ca. 1910 photo shows the lighthouse and the assistant keeper's quarters. *Courtesy of the US Coast Guard*

The Boca Grande Lighthouse, built in 1890, is located at the southern tip of Gasparilla Island. It was originally called the Gasparilla Island Light Station and marked the entry into Charlotte Harbor from the Gulf of Mexico. This lighthouse is the oldest building on Gasparilla Island, which is a 6-mile-long barrier island in Charlotte County. This lighthouse served both as a lighthouse keeper's home as well as an aid to navigation. It is a one-story building made of wood, sitting atop iron posts. About 70 feet away is an additional wood-frame structure that looks identical to this lighthouse except that it has no lantern room. This building housed the assistant lighthouse keeper and his family.

The light tower contains a black, octagon-shaped lantern structure. It is 44 feet tall and has sixty steps from the ground to the lantern room. Originally, a Third-order Fresnel lens was installed. Boca Grande was lit on December 31, 1890.

Before this barrier island was developed, life as a lighthouse keeper was lonely. Keepers used to entertain millionaires such as John D. Rockefeller and John Aster, who came to this area aboard their yachts to fish for tarpon. Since Charlotte Harbor was a deepwater port, and Boca Grande was at the end of a rail line, it became a state-of-the-art international shipping facility. Ships that transported phosphate to over twenty countries frequently docked at this lighthouse and port. This lighthouse also guided cattle ships that traveled from Charlotte Harbor to Cuba.

In World War II, the lighthouse guided US and Allied cargo ships into the harbor, where they sought refuge from German submarines located off the coast. The lighthouse became automated in 1956, and in 1966 the lantern was removed by the Coast Guard. They turned the building over to the US General Services Administration for disposal. Sadly, the lighthouse and the land surrounding it fell into disrepair. Erosion from the Gulf threatened its stability, and the structure began to lean. In 1972, it was turned over to Lee County. The local power company helped pump sand around the structure, and they built a rock groin along the shoreline to help with the erosion situation.

In 1980, it was placed on the National Register of Historic Places. The Gasparilla Island Conservation and Improvement Association restored the lighthouse, with the help of private citizens and the Florida Bureau of Historic Preservation. The State of Florida became the owner in 1988, and in 1999 it was opened to the public as the Boca Grande Lighthouse Museum. Although visitors cannot climb the lighthouse, they can visit a wonderful museum that is operated by the Barrier Island Parks Society, an all-volunteer group.

West Coast Lights: Cedar Key to Sanibel Island

Sanibel. Sanibel is known for its beaches and shelling.

SANIBEL ISLAND
(1884)

Sanibel Island is a beautiful barrier island off the coast of Fort Myers, known for its turquoise water and shelling. It is the only barrier island on the West Coast of Florida (not including the Panhandle) that has an east–west orientation. It is home to many famous people, including Mick Jagger, Dan Brown (author of *The Da Vinci Code*), retired newscaster Ted Koppel, retired NBC meteorologist Willard Scott, and, formerly, the late Walter Cronkite. Other historic visitors such as Thomas Edison and Henry Ford frequented Sanibel by passenger ferry before the causeway was built in 1963.

This tiny island is rich in history. It was first named "Sanybel" by a group of investors from New York, who established the first settlement in 1833. Their vision was cut short by frequent hurricanes and the threat of Indian attack during the Second Seminole War. By 1936, they abandoned "Sanybel" and returned north.

Sanibel. The 112-foot, skeleton pyramid tower was completed on August 20, 1884.

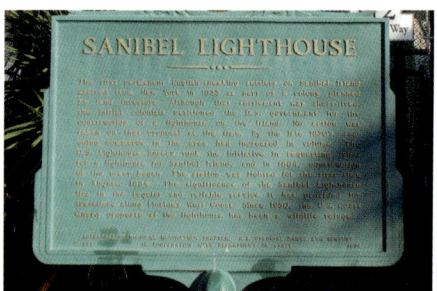

Left: Sanibel. There is a lighthouse exhibit at the Sanibel Historical Village. *Courtesy of J. Hyland*

Top: Historical marker. In 1974, the lighthouse and the keeper's quarters were added to the National Register of Historic Places.

From the 1830s to the Spanish-American War in 1898, as many as 16,000 cattle were shipped from Punta Rassa, a port on the opposite side of San Carlos Harbor, to Key West and Cuba. This lighthouse was critical due to the high volume of shipping traffic in this deepwater port and the fact that there were no lighthouses between Key West and Egmont Key, which is located off the coast of Tampa.

The Sanibel Island Lighthouse had a rough beginning. In 1883, Congress appropriated $50,000 to build this lighthouse. After the money was appropriated, Congress learned that the State of Florida owned the land, and so began a cumbersome process to transfer the land back to the federal government. The four-sided, skeletal pyramid tower (112 feet tall) was preassembled by Phoenix Ironworks in Ocean City, New Jersey, and was transported to Florida by ship. Unfortunately, the ship sank 2 miles away from Sanibel Island. Luckily, a diving crew salvaged most of the pieces along with the components for the Cape San Blas Lighthouse.

Construction on the lighthouse was completed on August 20, 1884. During construction, two wood-framed houses were also built on this land for the lighthouse keepers. They were erected on iron columns and were joined to the lighthouse by a stairway. A brick oil-storage house was added in 1894. These homes and the lighthouse are the oldest known structures on Sanibel Island.

In 1939, the US Coast Guard took over the operation and maintenance of the lighthouse. Shortly after this, the Coast Guard announced that this lighthouse would be closed since it was no longer of use. The residents organized a protest, and so the

Coast Guard. In 1939, the Coast Guard took over the operations and maintenance of the lighthouse. *Courtesy of the US Coast Guard*

lighthouse remained operational. In 1952, a TV antenna was placed on top of the tower, which allowed residents to watch television on the island for the very first time. The tower was converted to electricity in 1962. Twelve years later, the lighthouse and the keeper's quarters were added to the National Register of Historic Places. The Coast Guard relinquished responsibility for the lighthouse to the City of Sanibel. City workers live in the keeper's quarters and are responsible for maintaining the lighthouse and watching over the property.

The Sanibel Island lighthouse is located at the southeastern tip of the island. When crossing over the causeway, one can see it to the left of the bridge. The lighthouse is not open to the public, and there is no parking on the lighthouse grounds. However, there is a parking lot nearby with restrooms and a trail leading to the lighthouse. There is a lighthouse exhibit at the Sanibel Historical Village and Museum, along with a gift shop.

City of Sanibel. A 1933 photo shows very little development on Sanibel Island. *Courtesy of the US Coast Guard*

CHAPTER 7:
Panhandle Lights: Pensacola to St. Marks

The Panhandle of Florida is often referred to as the "Forgotten Coast." It is less populated and developed than other regions of Florida, but equally beautiful. Other than Tallahassee, the state's capital, and Pensacola, there are no other major cities here. Pensacola is the most populated city directly on the coast, followed by Panama City. Reminiscent of "old Florida," small towns dot the picturesque coast. Step onto the beaches of Destin or Panama City and you would think that you are in the Bahamas. White-sand beaches grace the coastline along the aqua waters of the Gulf of Mexico.

The deepwater seaport of Pensacola, on Pensacola Bay, is a major shipping port and is protected by the barrier island of Santa Rosa. Many lighthouses in the Panhandle are on barrier islands. The others are coastal lights that protect the harbors of small towns. They were strategically placed to assist mariners as they traveled close to the shoreline, bringing goods up from ports on the Atlantic or down from lumber or cotton merchants in the South. Today, numerous ships containing oil and other goods from the interior of America travel these waters regularly. The lights also guide recreational and commercial fisherman who call this place home. Residents are proud of their lighthouses and the important role they played in settling America.

Panhandle Lights: Pensacola to St. Marks

Pensacola. The 150-foot brick tower was completed and lit on January 1, 1859.

PENSACOLA
(1824, 1859)

In 1559, the Spaniards settled Pensacola and made it one the oldest European settlements in mainland America. Many other famous explorers charted Pensacola Bay, which was called Polonza. They were Ponce de León (1513), Pánfilo de Narváez (1528), and Hernando de Soto (1539).

Pensacola's strategic location has resulted in its being owned by several countries before it became part of America. Its nickname, "the City of Five Flags," comes from ownership by Britain, France (part of Louisiana), and Spain (Florida), followed by the Confederate States of America and, finally, the United States of America.

It was here that General Andrew Jackson, the first US governor of Florida, received the transfer from Spain. Soon after the United States took control from Spain in 1821, the Florida Territorial Legislature saw the need to protect Pensacola's harbor and sent a letter to President James Monroe requesting that a naval yard and lighthouse be built. In March 3, 1823, Congress passed an appropriation of

Spiral stairway. The stairway is 100 feet tall.

Brass and glass. Hundreds of glass prisms are held by a brass framework for the Fresnel lens.

$6,000 for the Pensacola Lighthouse. *Aurora Borealis*, a floating-light vessel from the mouth of the Mississippi, was moved to the western end of Santa Rosa Island to serve the port until the lighthouse was completed. It was the second lightship ever used in the United States.

The first keeper, Jeremiah Ingraham, first lit the lighthouse on December 20, 1824. It was a conical-shaped brick tower, 40 feet tall, with a 7-foot lantern. It was equipped with ten whale oil lamps, each flame enhanced with a 14-inch reflector. Two years later, Ingraham married Michaela Penalber of Pensacola and raised a family of three children here. When Keeper Ingraham passed away in 1840, Michaela took over the responsibility for the light.

In the late 1840s, the clockwork mechanism failed, and two men were hired to rotate the lamps by hand until repairs were made. Michaela served until she passed away in 1855. After her death, her son-in-law, Joseph Palmes, was appointed keeper.

Fresnel lens. Inside view of the First-order lens shows the electric lamp.

In 1850, ship captains complained that the light was too dim. The newly established Lighthouse Board recommended in 1852 that a "first-class seacoast light" with a height of no less than 150 feet be built there. Congress allocated $25,000 in 1854 and an additional $30,000 in 1856. A new site was selected one-half mile west of the original lighthouse, and work on the tower began. The 151-foot-tall tower was completed in 1858, and a First-order Fresnel lens was lit on New Year's Day in 1859. The tower was painted white, had a base diameter of 30 feet, and tapered to a diameter of 15 feet at the top.

On January 10, 1861, Florida seceded from the United States, and Confederates took control of the tower. They eventually discontinued the light and removed the lens. Confederates evacuated the area on May 9, 1862, and the lighthouse fell under Union control. In December 1861, shots from Fort Pickens hit the base of the light and damaged it in three places. Luckily, none of the rounds penetrated the outer wall of the lighthouse. A Fourth-order lens was placed in the lantern room, and the tower was relit on December 20, 1862.

Panhandle Light. This 1893 photograph shows the tallest lighthouse in the Panhandle.

After the Civil War, the original First-order Fresnel lens was recovered but was not reinstalled in the tower's lantern room until 1869. Also in 1869, a new keeper's quarters were built, and the tower's all-white day markings were changed. The bottom third of the tower remained white to contrast with surrounding trees, while the top was painted black to stand out against a cloudy sky. Lightning struck the lighthouse twice in 1875 and melted some of the metal fixtures.

In 1884, mineral oil lamps replaced the earlier lamps that burned whale oil, and in 1892 a brick oil house was built as a storage facility. A wooden shed was added in 1894 as a place to store empty oil cans. The frame addition to the keeper's quarters was converted to a kitchen, which connected the house to the lighthouse tower. A second story was also added to the keeper's porch in 1897.

Electricity was installed at the lighthouse and indoor plumbing was added to the keeper's quarters in October 1939. In 1953, Pensacola's last civilian lighthouse keeper, James Hatten, retired after twenty-two years of service (1931–1953), and the Coast Guard took over the keeper's duties. In 1965, it was fully automated, and the keeper's quarters were vacated.

The Pensacola Lighthouse was listed in the National Register of Historic Places in 1974, and in 1996 the US Coast Guard Auxiliary began public tours. The SyFy Channel's *Ghost Hunters* investigated the Pensacola Lighthouse in September 2009 and aired footage from this visit during their fifth season. The Travel Channel has also coined this lighthouse as "one of the most haunted in the nation."

In 2006, the Pensacola Lighthouse Association was established, and tours were turned over to this group. The lighthouse complex is on the Naval Air Station Pensacola base, so be prepared to pass through a security checkpoint. The famous Blue Angels are based out of this air station. The lighthouse offers a unique experience to witness the power of these jets on practice days.

A visit to the Pensacola Lighthouse can encompass an entire day. Visitors can climb the 177 steps for one of the most beautiful views of the Pensacola Pass, where Pensacola Bay meets the Gulf of Mexico. The restored keepers' quarters, which was built in 1869, houses the Richard C. Callaway Museum, which contains exhibits on local history and the lighthouse. Both are included with one admission ticket. There is also a nature trail near the lighthouse parking lot, which leads to a beautiful beach.

From the top of the lighthouse, one can see three historic forts, the Pensacola skyline, and the historic Navy Yard. Fort Barrancas, which was constructed between 1839 and 1844 to protect the Pensacola Navy Yard, is part of the National Park Service. It is also open for tours. Another attraction to include is the National Naval Aviation Museum, which is located across the street from the lighthouse. This free attraction is the world's largest navy aviation museum and is high on the list of "most visited museums in Florida."

The lighthouse complex is on the Naval Air Station Pensacola base, so be prepared to pass through a security checkpoint. The famous Blue Angels are based out of this air station. The lighthouse offers a unique experience to witness the power of these jets on practice days. Check the lighthouse website for more information on security and hours of operation.

Cape San Blas. In July 2014, the light was moved to Port St. Joe.

CAPE SAN BLAS
(1848, 1855, 1858, 1885)

Cape San Blas is a small town on the "Forgotten Coast" of Florida. It is located on a narrow peninsula, at the intersection of St. Joseph Bay Aquatic Preserve and the mainland of Florida. This spit separates the Gulf of Mexico on the south from St. Joseph Bay to the north. The Cape San Blas lighthouse can easily be nicknamed the "Bad Luck Lighthouse." Each time this lighthouse was built or rebuilt, something destroyed it.

It all began in 1848, when the first lighthouse was constructed. Three years later, on August 23, 1851, a hurricane destroyed it. It was rebuilt with $12,000 in federal funds and was relit by November 1855. On August 30, 1856, another hurricane, which was nicknamed "the Great Storm of 1856," wiped it out. The storm was so strong that it completely toppled the lighthouse and washed out the floor of the keeper's home, which was 8 feet above sea level. A lagoon now takes the place of the second San Blas lighthouse.

The third lighthouse, a brick tower that contained a Third-order Fresnel lens, was lit on May 1, 1858. Confederate troops captured it and burned the keeper's quarters. It was dark during the Civil War, and after major repairs, it was relit on July 23, 1865. A new keeper's house was built by 1870, which allowed better living quarters for the lighthouse keeper, who had been living in the base of the watchtower. Twelve years later, on July 3, 1882, the lighthouse was washed into the Gulf by erosion.

In 1883, plans for a fourth tower were made. A prefabricated iron skeletal tower was built, instead of like the one previously constructed of brick. It brought to Florida by ship, along with the Sanibel Lighthouse, when it was shipwrecked off the coast of Sanibel Island. Luckily, both towers were salvaged by divers. The tower was completed in February 1885, only 1,500 feet from the Gulf of Mexico. Within 10 years, the lighthouse was standing in the waters of the Gulf. By this time, one had to wonder if the Lighthouse Service was beginning to understand the concepts of shore erosion. The tower was moved 640 yards inland in 1918.

Steelwork. Looking up from the base of the 96-foot-tall steel tower.

The *Lighthouse Digest* magazine, which compiles a list of endangered lighthouses in their "Doomsday List," added Cape San Blas in June 2012. It was also added to the National Register of Historic Places in 2015.

In July 2014, it was moved to Core Park in the town of Port St. Joe, where it still stands today. Fascinating photos of this move can be seen on the lighthouse website. The light is now a white, square skeleton tower, with the lantern 96 feet above sea level. The compound also includes two two-story keeper's homes, each with six rooms, and the oil shed.

Cape San Blas

Left: Pond view. Great reflection of the Cape St. Blas Lighthouse.

Below: An 1892 photo. This was taken just shortly after the fourth tower was erected, much closer to the Gulf of Mexico. *Courtesy of the US Coast Guard*

Florida Lighthouses | 141

St. Joseph Point. In 1979, the light was moved to its current location and converted to a home.

ST. JOSEPH POINT
(1902, 1955)

The St. Joseph Bay Lighthouse may have met its demise in 1847, when another lighthouse (Cape San Blas) was built at the farther eastern point of the peninsula, but this was not the end of the story for the "traveling lighthouse." Although there were few people living on the mainland after a series of hurricanes and an outbreak of yellow fever, this bay still played an important role in commerce and American history.

As the only deepwater port between Tampa and Pensacola, it provided safe harbor for a large Gulf coast fishing fleet. In 1867, the Lighthouse Board decided that a lighthouse was necessary, and commissioned another light to be built on the mainland, directly opposite from the first lighthouse. President William McKinley signed the work order, and on July 1, 1898, Congress appropriated $15,000 to build this lighthouse in an area called Beacon Hill.

St. Joseph Point. Another early photo of the lighthouse prior to moving. *Courtesy of the US Coast Guard*

Work began on a new structure, which was named St. Joseph Light Range Station or St. Joseph Point Lighthouse. It was designed to be totally different than all the other Florida lighthouses. This one had a tower attached to a one-story, framed house, where the lighthouse keeper could live. Brick piers, 10 to 12 feet tall, supported this home, which had three bedrooms, a living room, and a combined kitchen and dining room. The watch room was built directly in the center of the building. A brick oil house was also added along with a 245-foot wharf. There were storerooms under the building for paint and other supplies. A cistern to catch rainwater was also built under the structure. Later, a well was drilled. A Third-order iron lantern, which projected a fixed white light out to 13 miles, was installed at 96 feet above sea level. This lighthouse, also nicknamed the Beacon Hill Light, was commissioned in 1902.

Later, during World War II, it played a major role in keeping America safe—Allied ships anchored in this harbor at night. Coast Guardsmen were stationed in barracks, which were set up beneath the family's living quarters at the lighthouse. Their job was to look for enemy U-boats and patrol the beaches at night to look for German spies, who used to sneak onshore during moonless nights from German subs. One night the beach patrol saw a German submarine surface, and reported it immediately to the senior officer at the lighthouse. A few days later it was torpedoed and sank.

Soldiers had to pass through the keeper's living quarters during this time, which made it interesting for Keeper Walter Roberts and his family. Historical documents found that his daughters used to iron the soldiers' uniforms for 10 cents each, and the keeper's sons used to polish their boots.

In 1955, a 78-foot iron skeleton tower with an automated light replaced it. Five years later, it was classified as surplus and auctioned for $300. It was moved 3 miles to Overstreet Highway and used as a home for its first owner. Sam Harmon, the second owner, used it as a barn and actually fed cows from the porch. Danny Raffield bought it in 1970 for $1,200 but did not move it the 23 miles west to Summons Bayou until 1979. After extensive renovations, it was converted to a private home.

Along with the lighthouse, there is a marble monument containing the names of the delegates from the Constitutional Convention in Port St. Joe on Monument Avenue. There is also a museum at this site.

A 1950 photo. An aerial view shows the lighthouse prior to its moving. *Courtesy of the US Coast Guard*

Cape St. George. The fourth lighthouse, constructed in 2008.

CAPE ST. GEORGE
(1833, 1847, 1852, 2008)

Off the coast of Apalachicola sits a long barrier island called St. George Island. Hurricanes and other storms over the years have made it difficult for lighthouses to remain. The Cape St. George Lighthouse is actually the fourth lighthouse on this island. The first one was built in 1833 on the western part of the island, at West Pass. Since ships couldn't actually see the light until they were in shallow, dangerous water, it had to be dismantled. The second light was built on the southernmost tip of the island in 1848, but it was destroyed in 1851 by a hurricane.

The third lighthouse, built in 1852, sits 250 yards inland from the second lighthouse. The builder used approximately two-thirds of the bricks from the 1847 lighthouse. The base was 20 feet across, and at the top the diameter was 12 feet. The walls were solid brick, 4 feet thick at the bottom and 2 feet at the top. The top of the lighthouse had a soapstone deck that was 5 inches thick. The day markings were white on the bottom with a black tower. It stood 74 feet tall. In 1857, a Third-order Fresnel lens was installed that could be seen 14 miles out to sea.

Cape St. George. After the collapse of the third lighthouse in 2005, a new one was built, reusing 22,000 bricks.

Tower and fireplace. A 2001 photo taken prior to the demise of the third lighthouse. *Courtesy of the Cape St. George Lighthouse Society*

As with many lighthouses in Florida, Confederate troops occupied this lighthouse during the Civil War, and the lighthouse went dark to keep Union troops from finding this outpost. The lens and other valuable parts were removed for safekeeping and stored off-site. This particular lens was damaged during war and had to be replaced with another in 1889. Oil was the main source of fuel, followed by electricity from a gas-powered generator. Eventually, as with most lighthouses of this time, the Fresnel lens was replaced by a more modern lens and then became automated. This era marked the end of the need for lighthouse keepers.

In 1995, Hurricane Opal made a direct hit on this part of the Panhandle. It severely weakened the foundation of the lighthouse, and the entire structure started to lean at a 7.5-degree angle. The hurricane also demolished the keeper's home and the oil storage house. Since neither were actually needed in the 1990s, the newly formed Cape St. George Lighthouse Society raised funds to restore the damaged light and try to stabilize it. Eventually, it settled back into a vertical position, but not for long. By 2004, the lighthouse was completely surrounded by Gulf waters, and wind and erosion continued to destabilize it.

Water surrounding the tower after the storm. *Courtesy of the Cape St. George Lighthouse Society*

On October 21, 2005, this historic lighthouse totally collapsed. A huge group of volunteers, contractors, and government workers scrambled to salvage as many pieces of the lighthouse as possible. They placed them is a storage facility on the mainland, where volunteers gathered on the weekends to clean off the mortar of more than 22,000 bricks. The bricks along with granite door jambs and window lintels from the 1852 light were used to build the fourth lighthouse. It was completed in December 2008 and still stands today. A replica of the keeper's quarters was built and now houses a small museum and gift shop.

Healthy dune. A 1950 photograph shows a healthy dune surrounding the lighthouse. *Courtesy of the US Coast Guard*

Collapsed tower. On October 21, 2005, the lighthouse fell into the Gulf of Mexico. *Courtesy of the Cape St. George Lighthouse Society*

Cape St. George

Leaning tower—just days before the tower collapsed. *Courtesy of the Cape St. George Lighthouse Society*

Crooked River. The first tower was constructed in 1839 and was destroyed in 1873.

CROOKED RIVER
(1839, 1895)

The Crooked River Lighthouse is tucked away from the main road going west of the quiet town of Carrabelle. Before it was positioned here, it was located on Dog Island, a nearby barrier island. Dog Island (Isles aux Chiens) was first named by the French who explored this area. They found packs of wild dogs living there, and they say that the 7-mile island was shaped like a dog. This barrier island sits at the mouth St. George's Sound and provides safe harbor for Carrabelle.

Because of its location, Dog Island was a strategic place for a lighthouse. The first light was built in 1839 on the western end of the island. It was damaged by storms in the 1840s and again during the Civil War. Since it was positioned in an area with no protection from the wind and waves, storms continued to damage the light from 1872 to 1873. In 1873, a hurricane destroyed both the lighthouse and the keeper's quarters.

Campers' companion. "Bodie the Wonder Dog" traveled with us to photograph the lighthouses of Florida.

Although Congress approved a $20,000 appropriation to rebuild the lighthouse and the keeper's quarters, it was never built. Some officials deemed it unnecessary due to the lack of trade and commerce in the area. Later in the 1880s, the lumber trade from the Apalachicola and the Crooked Rivers warranted another appropriation of $40,000. After a land title issue was resolved, construction of the Crooked River Lighthouse, now on the mainland, began. It was completed in August 1895 and was lit on October 28. Today this light sits at 115 feet above sea level and contains a Fourth-order Fresnel lens. It is painted red on the top and white on the bottom to set it apart from the surrounding pine trees.

An active Carrabelle Lighthouse Association has restored the lighthouse and operates a gift shop and a small museum.

Right: Crooked River, ca. 1890 photograph. *Courtesy of the US Coast Guard*

Below: The keeper's quarters are now a museum and gift shop.

Crooked River

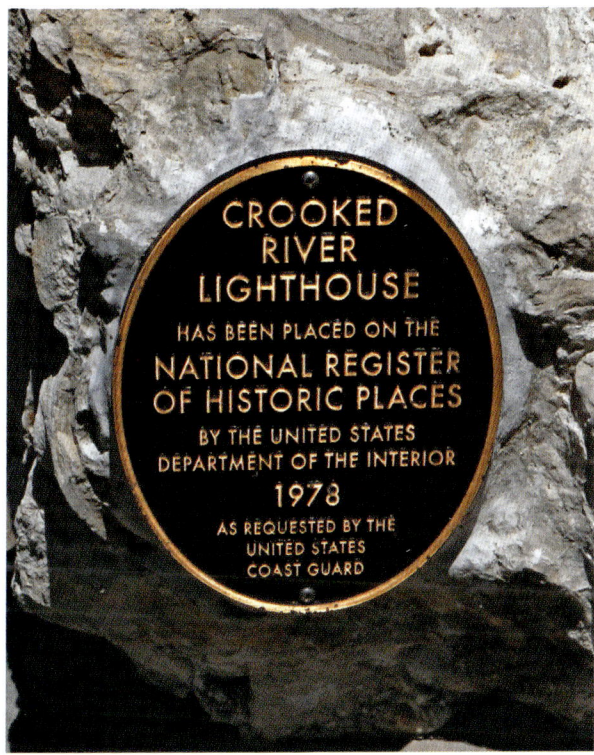

Left: In 1978, the Crooked River Lighthouse was placed in the National Register of Historic Places.

Below: Dock, lighthouse, and keeper's quarters, ca. 1900 photograph. *Courtesy of the US Coast Guard*

Florida Lighthouses | 155

Panhandle Lights: Pensacola to St. Marks

St. Marks. The 82-foot lighthouse was completed in 1842.

ST. MARKS LIGHT STATION
(1837, 1842)

St. Marks Light Station is the second-oldest existing lighthouse in Florida. Located 25 miles south of Tallahassee, St. Marks is situated in the Big Bend region of Florida, where the coastline of the Gulf changes from a north–south direction to east–west. St. Marks is located on the east side of the St. Marks River on Apalachee Bay. The Spanish first settled this beautiful area. In 1818, Andrew Jackson captured St. Marks from the Spanish, and three years later, control of Florida was officially transferred from Spain to the United States.

In 1828, William P. Duval, who succeeded Andrew Jackson as governor of the Florida Territory, petitioned Congress for the construction of a lighthouse at St. Marks. On May 23, 1828, $6,000 was appropriated for the construction of the lighthouse. When it seemed that this was not enough to cover construction, $14,000 was appropriated. The final cost of construction was $11,765. The first lighthouse was built with hollow walls, which was not acceptable to the collector of customs. Later, a solid replacement tower was constructed and commissioned in 1830. St.

St. Marks. This lighthouse is located in St. Marks National Wildlife Refuge, a 68,000-acre park.

St. Marks. A 1913 photograph of the keeper's quarters and lighthouse.

Marks stands 73 feet tall and projects a fixed white light from fifteen lamps set in 15-inch reflectors.

As this port became more popular with farmers from Florida and Georgia, cotton growers financed a 20-mile-long railroad. The Tallahassee–St. Marks Railroad, Florida's first railroad, was built in 1837. Mules initially pulled it until 1850, when locomotives were purchased. The port continued to grow but the surrounding land began to shrink. By 1842, a new lighthouse was built farther inland. The third lighthouse, which is still standing today, rests on a bed of local limestone. The walls are 4 feet thick at the bottom and 18 inches at the top.

This lighthouse was battered many times by storms and hurricanes. It saved the lives of Keeper John Hungerford and his family in 1843. After this hurricane, a breakwater was built to protect the lighthouse. The hurricane of 1851 struck but the tower withstood this fierce storm very well, even though the keeper's home was severely damaged. The home had to be replaced in 1854, along with a new foundation for the lighthouse and a breakwater.

Storms were not the only enemy of the lighthouse. Prior to the Civil War, the customs collector removed all the valuables from the property, and both sides of the conflict used the lighthouse. Confederate forces first used the dwelling as a barracks and a fortress. The tower served as a lookout. Union ships bombarded the lighthouse on June 15, 1862, and a year later, Union sailors returned and burned the wooden steps in the tower to prevent Confederates from spying on their activities. When Union forces landed near the lighthouse in 1865 to march on Tallahassee, they discovered that the retreating Confederates had burned the dwelling and set off multiple charges in holes they had drilled in the tower. One blast tore an 8-foot hole in the tower, while other blasts succeeded only in dislodging several outer layers of brick from the tower.

When the war was over, the tower was repaired between September and December 1866, and a new Fourth-order Fresnel lens was installed in the lantern room, allowing Keeper David Kennedy to return to the post he had briefly held before the war. He placed the light back in operation on January 7, 1867.

Another hurricane struck in 1873, forcing the keepers' families to seek shelter in the tower. The keeper's house sustained major damage, and the concrete around the tower's foundation also needed to be repaired.

This lighthouse was later incorporated into St. Marks National Wildlife Refuge, a beautiful winter habitat for migrating birds, spanning more than 68,000 acres. In 1939, the Coast Guard became responsible for all the lighthouses in the nation. The keeper's son, Alton Grisham, joined the Coast Guard and was assigned to St. Marks, where he served until it was automated in 1960.

The Coast Guard spent $150,000 in 2000 to repair and stabilize the lighthouse. In June 2006, Congress passed an act that transferred the lighthouse and the surrounding 8 acres from the Coast Guard to the US Fish and Wildlife Service. The transfer did not take place until October 2013 because lead-contaminated soil around the lighthouse had to be removed. On March 28, 2014, an official transfer ceremony was held that included descendants of the lighthouse keepers. In November 2014, the US Fish and Wildlife Service had the Fresnel lens removed so the lantern room could be restored. It was transported to Ponce de Leon Inlet Lighthouse, where a team of volunteers spent over five hundred hours cleaning it. The following March, the lens was placed on display in St. Marks National Wildlife Refuge's visitors center.

On March 17, 2016, Governor Rick Scott signed the 2016 General Appropriations Act, which allocated a total of $550,000 for the St. Marks Lighthouse. Fifty thousand dollars was used to restore the lantern room, and $500,000 for preserving the lighthouse itself. St. Marks Lighthouse was the location for the music video "The Lighthouse Tale," on lighthouse keepers in the 1850s. After seeing the beautiful lighthouse complex, visitors can stop at the wildlife refuge's visitors center, which is open seven days a week and contains many lighthouse items.

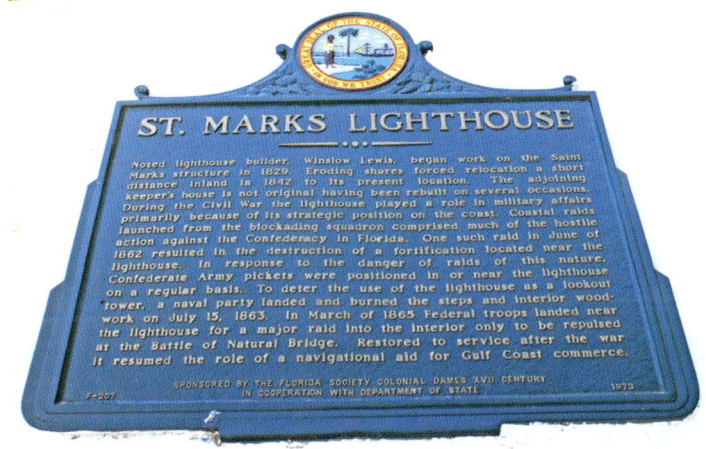

Historical marker. The State of Florida prepared this marker in 1973.

CHAPTER 8:
Lost Beacons of Florida

Lost beacons are an important part of Florida's maritime history. Some were lighthouses and others were range lights. Range lights are nautical markers, used in succession, to guide ships into narrow bodies of water.

Some of these beacons were demolished out of disrepair. The saltwater life takes its toll on man-made structures, and lighthouses are no exception. Others were taken out of service during the Civil War. Most were the victims of destructive forces of nature, such as lightning, hurricanes, and storm surge. In some cases, there are no remnants of the lighthouse. In other cases, although the light is gone, there is a simple tower or marker containing National Oceanographic and Atmospheric Administration (NOAA) weather equipment or a flashing light. These skeletons mark places where these beacons used to stand. Although these lighthouses are gone, they are not forgotten.

Amelia Island North Range. This 1880 photo shows a wood-framed keeper's house and tower. *Courtesy of the US Coast Guard*

AMELIA ISLAND NORTH RANGE
(1859)

In 1859, two additional lights were needed to mark the entrance to St. Mary's Channel. The front tower was the smaller of the two beacons. To the west was a small, Sixth-order red Fresnel lens, positioned on top of the wood-framed keeper's house. During the Civil War, the lens was removed for safekeeping. In March 1862, Union troops seized the town of Fernandina, and the lighthouse was demolished. In late 1871, construction began, and the rear range tower consisted of a lantern on a framed house. Because of shifting sand, the entrance of the channel required that both lights be placed on tramways in 1887. The lighthouse was discontinued in 1899, and buoys were used to mark the channel. Surveys of Amelia Island showed the lighthouse along the shore in 1924.

Lost Beacons of Florida

Charlotte Harbor (1900). This lighthouse was located in the shallow bay of Charlotte Harbor and was manned by a keeper and an assistant. *Courtesy of the US Coast Guard*

CHARLOTTE HARBOR
(1890)

Charlotte Harbor, a large, shallow bay on Florida's West Coast, was never suited for major seagoing ships. However, when the railroad came to Punta Gorda, it became a major shipping port for cattle. In 1890, the Charlotte Harbor Lighthouse was built in 9 feet of water at the center of the bay. It was constructed at the same time as the similar Gasparilla Island Lighthouse. The light was a wooden house-like structure, set on iron pilings, with a lantern on top. It was painted white with green shutters and had a red roof. A keeper and an assistant manned the flashing white light.

Since this lighthouse was located southeast of Cape Haze, it was sometimes called the "Cape Haze Lighthouse." In 1911, the light was converted to acetylene gas, and it was unmanned by 1918. The light remained active until the 1930s. After years of neglect, the light was badly weathered and was torn down in 1943. It was replaced with an iron skeletal tower, and later it became Charlotte Harbor Light Six, a triangular day board located where the former lighthouse had stood.

Dames Point (1876). One of the only river lighthouses in Florida, it was preceded by a lightship. *Courtesy of the US Coast Guard*

DAMES POINT
(1872)

Dames Point Lighthouse was one of the only river lighthouses in Florida. It was located in a 12-foot shoal in the St. Johns River. A small lightship first marked the site in 1857. The lightship was manned by a crew of three: the captain, a cook, and one crewman. During the Civil War, the lightship was towed to Jacksonville. A Confederate fort (at Yellow Bluff) guarded Dames Point Shoal. The Yellow Bluff Fort was abandoned in 1863, and Jacksonville was later occupied by Union troops. By 1870, shipping increased and there was a need to build a lighthouse on the shoal. After the lighthouse was framed in Maryland, it was disassembled, shipped south, and reassembled on wooden piles at Dames Point.

In 1875, Napoleon Broward, the future governor of Florida, lived in the lighthouse while attending school in New Berlin. Lightning stuck the tower several times in 1891. In 1892, the light was discontinued and the top of the lighthouse was removed and used in another location. The remaining lighthouse was destroyed in a fire in 1913.

Dog Island. On September 8, 1873, a hurricane swept away the tower and the keeper's house.
Courtesy of the US Coast Guard

DOG ISLAND
(1839)

Dog Island, at the eastern pass to St. George Sound and Apalachicola Bay, received a lighthouse in 1839. It was 44 feet tall, made of brick, and painted white. The lantern contained a Fourth-order lens, which was visible for 13 miles and revolved to help distinguish it from the Cape St. George Lighthouse.

In October 1843, a hurricane destroyed the keeper's house and badly damaged the tower.

A great storm hit in 1851, which swept away the door of the lighthouse, killing five people, and cut a channel through Dog Island. After the lighthouse was destroyed, a new one was built the following year.

Beach erosion played a large part in the tower leaning over 1 foot from perpendicular.

In 1872, the lantern was removed to the top of the keeper's dwelling, which was set back from the shore. On September 18, 1873, a hurricane washed both the tower and dwelling into St. George Sound. Fortunately, the keeper and the assistant survived, but the lighthouse was never rebuilt. The only remains of this light are a pile of bricks offshore.

Ft. Barrancus Rear Range (1892). In one of the three forts to guard Pensacola Bay, this range light was built in 1855. *Courtesy of the US Coast Guard*

FORT BARRANCUS REAR RANGE
(1855)

The Fort Barrancus Rear Range lights were constructed in 1855 to mark the entrance of the channel at Pensacola Bay. They were extinguished two years later at the start of the Civil War. In 1867, the range lights were relit after a delay caused by the failure of the keeper to report for duty. Eleven months later, they were discontinued since it was felt they were no longer necessary. The range lights were reestablished in 1888 near the site of the first Pensacola Lighthouse. The rear light was located on a wooden frame with a small two-room house for the keeper. The home was enlarged to include a kitchen and dining room in 1897. Keeper William Doyle was one of twenty lighthouse keepers along the Gulf coast who were commended for "performing their duties under hazardous and unusual conditions" during the hurricane of 1917. The Fort Barrancas Range Lights were unmanned by 1920 and discontinued in 1930.

FORT MCREE REAR RANGE LIGHTS
(1859)

There were three forts that guarded the entrance to Pensacola Bay before the Civil War: Fort McRee, Fort Pickens, and Fort Barrancus. A set of range lights were built in 1859 just south of Fort McRee to guide vessels into the harbor. When the Civil War started, Union troops abandoned Forts McRee and Barrancus and fled to Fort Pickens. After severe bombing of Fort McRee, it was turned into a pile of rubble. After the Civil War, the lights were reestablished in 1866, but they were destroyed again in a hurricane. In 1906, the Fort McRee Rear Range Light was replaced by the Fort McRee Cutoff Range, which acted in combination with the Caucus Cut Range, the Fort Barrancas Range, and the Pensacola Range. The hurricanes of 1916 and 1917 caused minor damage to the lights. In 1918, the station was automated. The ruins of Fort McRee were visible until the 1930s.

Ft. McRee-Caucus Range (1892). In 1918, the lighthouse was automated. *Courtesy of the US Coast Guard*

Top: Ft. McRee-Caucus Range. The ruins of the fort were visible until the 1930s. *Courtesy of the US Coast Guard*

Molasses Reef. An unmanned reef lighthouse was built in 1927. *Courtesy of the US Coast Guard*

MOLASSES REEF
(1921)

Many unmanned reef lights on the Florida Keys were erected between 1921 and 1935. These lights were designed to be automated and resembled the older reef lights, which had a skeletal pyramidal upper structure on a screw-pile foundation. Originally, they all had lanterns on their peaks, so they resembled smaller versions of the older reef lights. These reef lights had no keepers' quarters. The Molasses Reef Light was erected in 1927 as a brown, square pyramidal skeleton on a pile foundation. The skeleton is still standing but the lantern has been removed. An automatic NOAA weather station sits at the top of the tower, which is painted brown and stands in 9 feet of water.

Lost Beacons of Florida

Molasses Reef. An automatic NOAA weather station sits on top of the tower.
Courtesy of the US Coast Guard

MOSQUITO INLET
(1835)

Mosquito Inlet, which is known today as Ponce Inlet, has been recognized as one of the most hazardous inlets on the East Coast of Florida. The British erected a day beacon on the north side of the inlet in 1774. In 1834, Congress authorized $11,000 for the construction of a lighthouse on the south side of the inlet. The lighthouse was constructed by Winslow Lewis for $7,494 and outfitted with eleven of Lewis's patented 14-inch reflectors. On February 2, 1835, the keeper's dwelling was completed.

A hurricane struck in 1835; the storm did little damage to any of the structures but damaged some of the glass panes in the lantern room. However, the keeper wanted to protect the delicate lamps and removed them to the security of his dwelling. In October, during a high gale, the keeper's quarters were destroyed, and the base of the lighthouse began to erode. The keeper fled with his family to a nearby plantation.

Later in 1835, during the Second Seminole War, the Seminoles attacked plantations and burned down New Smyrna. The Indians marched to the peninsula and the Mosquito Inlet Lighthouse, smashed the rest of the glass, and set fire to the wooden parts of the lighthouse. Because of the problems with the Indians, the engineers could not get to the lighthouse to repair it. In April 1836, the foundation completely eroded, and the lighthouse collapsed into the inlet. This was the first lighthouse attack by the Indians in North America.

NORTHWEST PASSAGE (1839)

Northwest Passage. This 1892 photograph shows the fully operational lighthouse, which was automated in 1913. *Courtesy of the US Coast Guard*

The last remaining trace of this lighthouse is seen on current charts by the notation "Platform (in ruins)." The epitaph tells little of the life experience of those who built the Northwest Passage Lighthouse. The natural channel was noted in the 1842 edition of the *American Coast Pilot*, a publication that contained directions for the principal harbors and headlines on the coasts of North and South America. It stated, "There is passage through Key West from the Florida Stream, into the Bay of Mexico for vessels drawing 12 feet of water. The channel offers the only navigable route in the area."

On March 3, 1853, Congress appropriated $12,000 for a lighthouse to be built on iron piles to take the place of the lightship at Northwest Passage. The wooden house and iron-pile foundation were built in Philadelphia and shipped to Key West in May 1854. Due to the outbreak of yellow fever in Key West, several mechanics became sick and were sent back to Philadelphia. Another group returned in October to finish construction. William Richard, who had been the keeper at the Key West Lighthouse, lit the Fifth-order Fresnel lens for the first time on March 5, 1855. The light was visible over 275 degrees of the horizon and had a visible range of 10 miles beyond the bar.

Maintenance issues increased in the 1870s from corrosion and rotten woodwork. In 1878, $6,000 was requested to make the necessary repairs and replace the rotting woodwork. A new Fourth-order lens at an increased height of 47 feet was relit on June 30, 1879. The hurricane of 1909 battered the light with winds up to 130 mph, and a 12-foot storm surge caused major damage to the braces in the lighthouse foundation. The repairs were made to the foundation. In September 1913, a fire broke out on the platform, and by October 1913 the light was automated and the keeper's position was discontinued. In 1970, the Northwest Passage Lighthouse was declared a Florida landmark by the Association of American Architects. On August 30, 1971, the Northwest Passage Lighthouse was destroyed by fire.

Lost Beacons of Florida

Pulaski Shoal. The light was built in 1943 and was located 30 miles northwest of Key West.
Courtesy of the US Coast Guard

PULASKI SHOAL
(1935)

The Pulaski Shoal Light was one of two lights built in 1943, using the 1932 pile design. It was located 30 miles northwest of Key West and north of Dry Tortugas. The lighthouse stood in 15 feet of water, was painted black, and was 35 feet tall. As of September 2017, the NOAA Data Buoy Center reports an active automated weather station at this location, but no lighthouse.

REBECCA SHOAL
(1886)

The Rebecca Shoal was the last lighthouse to be built in the Florida Keys. It was one of the most difficult to erect because of the turbulent waters in the area. Rebecca Shoal lies 43 miles west of Key West in 11 feet of water. The swift Gulf Stream current flows north in high tide at about 1 knot, ebbs at a little less than a knot, and is greatly influenced by the wind. Because of the dimensions of the Gulf, the waves do not always move back and forth through the basin twice a day. There are differences in tidal patterns between the Gulf and Atlantic Ocean that contribute to the confusion of the seas where the waters join.

Rebecca Shoal. A 1900 photograph of a crew on the deck of Rebecca Shoal. *Courtesy of the US Coast Guard*

The seas around Rebecca Shoal are always turbulent. In May 1886, a working platform was built. After multiple attempts, countless delays, and two appropriations, the work was completed at Rebecca Shoal, and the lighthouse was lit on November 1, 1886. The first keeper was Mark Gage, who served both on Fowey Rocks and Carysfort Reef lighthouses. During stormy weather in 1887, the deck was badly damaged. The following year, a new deck was delivered and installed. From 1902 to 1903, the lighthouse was affected by storms and a series of unfortunate incidents.

On Friday, April 18, at 1:30 p.m., the lighthouse keeper was still at his station. By that Monday, he disappeared from the station. No one knows if he fell or jumped overboard. His body was never recovered.

On July 28, 1925, a historic move was reported by the *Key West Citizen*. The lighthouse was changed from a vapor-type light to an acetylene type, which eliminated the need for a keeper. The light was fully automated on August 1, 1944, and in December 1944, the planning officer of the Coast Guard recommended that the light by electrified. The keeper's house was removed in 1953, and a small, square, skeletal white tower on a brown platform was built with acetylene equipment. In 1985, the acetylene beacon was replaced with a modern, solar-powered, 190-millimeter rotating optic.

Volusia Bar (1915). Located at the entrance to the St. Johns River, a light was needed to direct the fifty or more steamers that traveled between Jacksonville and Lake George. *Courtesy of the US Coast Guard*

VOLUSIA BAR
(1886)

In the 1880s, about fifty steamers regularly made the Jacksonville–Sanford run through Lake George and Lake Monroe. In March 1883, the Lighthouse Board requested that Congress authorize a lighthouse at the southern end of Lake George, which sits at the entrance to the St. Johns River at Volusia Bar. This lighthouse would cost $5,000 and benefit 40,000 people and five counties who depend on ships that navigate Volusia Bar.

In early February 1885, B. P. Lamberton, inspector of the Sixth District, wrote to the chairman of the Lighthouse Board and sent blueprints for the new lighthouse. He agreed that a main light was needed, and suggested that range lights were also needed. In the fall of 1885, iron piles and framework were brought down from Baltimore and were set in 4.5 feet of water. The dwelling was prefabricated in Charleston and included a Fourth-order lens for the lantern room. It included a large bell that served as a fog signal and also served as a once-a-week mail drop-off for the local residents. It was completed in March 1886.

The original Fourth-order fixed Fresnel was replaced in 1899 with a Fifth-order lens. In 1908, the lantern at Volusia Bar Lighthouse was deactivated and the station was downgraded to just a fog signal. After several severe freezes had reduced agricultural shipping to a minimum, the expanding railroad system took over most of the passenger and freight needs. Steamboat traffic greatly decreased on the St. Johns River, and the golden age of steam boating in Florida was over.

In 1938, a fog signal was installed, and the light attendant was A. J. Anderson. That winter, the local residents noticed that the lamps were not being lit. When they went to investigate, they found Anderson's body floating in the water. The lighthouse was ransacked, and signs of a struggle were everywhere. A gruesome trail of blood led from the bedroom to the porch and to the dock. The *Daytona Beach News Journal* reported that the local residents had their suspicions about Anderson's death. A federal investigator was sent to help with the case, and Anderson was buried in a pauper's grave. The state attorney general obtained a court order to exhume the body, and the coroner examined the body at the gravesite. It was determined that Anderson had not been shot or stabbed, but his neck was broken by "causes unknown." The mystery surrounding his death still remains.

The bell was replaced with an electric horn in 1939, and in 1943 the lighthouse was discontinued. The abandoned lighthouse was a popular fishing camp and used as a summer residence for a local family. By 1954, the structure had deteriorated. It was damaged by a hurricane in 1964, and in the early 1970s it was burned by vandals. The iron legs of this lighthouse are the only remaining hardware to mark its location.

Volusia Bar. A Fifth-order lens was place in 1899, and in 1908 the light was downgraded to a fog signal.
Courtesy of the US Coast Guard

CHAPTER 9:
Preserving Lighthouses and Maritime History in Florida and America

There are over seven hundred lighthouses in America, thirty of which are located in Florida. To preserve a lighthouse is to preserve an important piece of American and maritime history. When ships were the primary means of transportation in early America, lighthouses served mariners well. Over the years, people were transported by stagecoach, trains, automobiles, buses, and, now, airplanes. Most goods are transported by trains and trucks. The shipping trade, while still vibrant today, does not rely solely on lighthouses or lightships as an aid to navigation. Advanced global-positioning technologies and radar have replaced the dependence on lighthouses.

In the late 1800s, as technology became more advanced, the power sources that were used to light the lamps evolved from fuels (whale oil or lard oil) to electricity. The first lighthouse to be electrified was a science experiment by Thomas Edison in 1886. Edison powered the Statue of Liberty in New York Harbor with direct current. The light source was returned to fuel when the generator failed. Throughout the early 1900s, many lighthouses were converted to electric power. The machinery that rotated lenses in the towers also became automated and powered by electricity.

The installation of these technologies replaced the need for a lighthouse keeper and his assistant. From 1968 to 1989, the US Coast Guard proposed the Lighthouse Automation Modernization Program (LAMP) to accelerate automation and standardize the remaining lighthouses in the United States. Some of the keepers went on to join the Coast Guard and stayed in their chosen occupation.

As they transitioned to being automated, many lighthouses became part of a state or national park. Others, such as Cape Lookout or Hatteras in North Carolina, became part of a national seashore. The Coast Guard worked with nonprofit preservation groups to develop long-term agreements so that the lighthouses, adjacent buildings, and the land could be transferred and maintained. Upon demonstrating good stewardship following a trial period, the Coast Guard would deed the property to a preservation group. Some of the lights were converted to interesting maritime museums that are filled with lighthouse artifacts. The remainder of the smaller lighthouses were inventoried and sold at public auction.

As keepers were phased out, a part of history was at risk of being lost forever. For many years, keepers diligently kept a lighthouse logbook. These men and women were valuable historians through their logs. In Florida, many lighthouses struggled to keep their keepers until the 1950s, while many were let go in the early 1900s.

The lovers of lighthouses and everything nautical saw the need to preserve this important part of American history. Preservation groups were formed for many of the lighthouses, and several national nonprofits were established to support the local communities in their preservation efforts.

As an owner of a lighthouse, local preservation groups face many challenges. All the Florida lighthouses are located in extremely windy and corrosive environments. Many structures and apparatus are over a hundred years old and need special craftsmen to repair or preserve them. They are subject to the nation's nastiest hurricanes, which subject them to wind, salt water, and tidal surge. Whether the lighthouse is tall, such as Ponce Inlet at 175 feet, or shorter, such as St. Marks, all require constant attention to building and land maintenance. The cost of annual repair is a constant challenge for these groups as they work to ensure that these national treasures will be kept for future generations.

In the state of Florida, the Florida Lighthouse Association was formed to advocate for preserving Florida's remaining lighthouses. This all-volunteer organization meets quarterly and operates under the umbrella of the US Lighthouse Society. They have great passion for preserving, restoring, protecting, and defending Florida lighthouses. On an annual basis, they review and approve grants totaling over $100,000. Most of the thirty lighthouses have their own group who support them. We urge you to visit all the lighthouses in Florida and "adopt" the lighthouse that is closest to you. These groups are always looking for dedicated volunteers to help manage their facility or help raise support.

There are two national groups that have been working diligently to support the lighthouses in America through funding, lobbying Congress, and providing source material for local lighthouse preservation societies. These are the Lighthouse Preservation Society and the US Lighthouse Society.

The Lighthouse Preservation Society is a nonprofit organization, founded by Jay Hyland and based in Massachusetts. They have made lighthouse preservation a national issue, with congressional hearings, conferences, the sponsorship of National Lighthouse Day and its celebrations, the nomination of twenty-five US lighthouse stamps, and the raising of nearly $6 million for over 160 lighthouse projects. This prestigious group is also the recipient of a Presidential Achievement Award from the federal government for its efforts to preserve America's lighthouse heritage.

The US Lighthouse Society is a nonprofit dedicated to being a primary source for lighthouse heritage information. They are a leader in lighthouse-related education, and they publish a quarterly newsletter, the *Keeper's Log*. They operate a speaker's bureau and maintain vast archival information on their website. They also offer domestic and international trips to tour lighthouses.

KEEPER'S LOG

In the early years of lighthouses, keepers did only manual labor. Lighthouse keepers were required after 1872 to post a daily log in a ledger, which was supplied by the Lighthouse Service. Their tasks now required them to read and write. The instructions for keeping the log were pasted on the inside front cover of the log, and keepers interpreted them in many different ways. Most recorded only the weather, while others included details about cleaning and repairing the station Some identified every ship that passed by or supply boat that arrived. Others included personal information such as family illnesses, school achievements, or church attendance.

All keepers recorded disasters such as ships going aground or seamen drowning. Many logs also contained pasted newspaper clippings. Personal letters were commonly found between pages. While some keepers wrote their names at the top or bottom of each entry, others never identified themselves at all.

Visitors to the lighthouses are encouraged to view samples of the keepers' logs in the maritime and lighthouse museums around the state. These logs are truly as individual as the keepers. Reading one is much like reading a history book. Each contains a unique and interesting account of a keeper's life, including challenges of living with their family there, weathering great storms, and other local history.

Appendixes

Listed in the appendixes are maps, guides, and handbooks for various Florida lighthouses. There are national, state, and local preservation groups, should you wish to support them and volunteer. As always, another great source of supplemental material may be found on various internet sites. Most lighthouses have their own home page, containing historical information, cost for tours, hours of operation, and directions for travel.

APPENDIX 1: MAPS, GUIDES, AND HANDBOOKS

1. *Lighthouses of the United States*—An illustrated map and directory to all standing lighthouses in the United States. Hartnett House Publishers.

2. *America's Atlantic Coast Lighthouses*—Contains directions to lighthouses located in thirteen states along the Atlantic Ocean. Written by Kenneth Kochel.

3. *Florida Lighthouses*—Contains local maps and information on all of Florida's lighthouses. Written by Kevin M. McCarthy.

4. *Florida Atlas and Gazetteer*—If you prefer a hardcopy map, this is the definitive guide to Florida, containing back roads, campgrounds, museums, theme parks, and more. DeLorme Publishers.

5. *Florida Lighthouses: Illustrated Map & Guide*—Map, short history, lighthouse and maritime museums, and illustrations. Bella Terra Publishing.

6. *Maritime Museums of North America*—A great reference for finding information on America's maritime history. Written by Robert Smith.

7. *A Listing of All Existing US Lighthouses*—A great checklist to use as you plan your lighthouse visits. Written by Bob and Sandra Shaklin.

APPENDIX 2: UNIQUE FLORIDA LIGHTHOUSE FACTS

Florida, with 30 lighthouses, ranks seventh in the nation in the number of lighthouses that are still standing. Michigan is first in the country with 116 lighthouses. There are nineteen states which have no lighthouses at all.

Tallest Tower: Ponce de Leon Inlet Lighthouse is 175 feet and the second tallest in America.

Highest Focal Plane: The Pensacola Lighthouse has a focal plane of 195 feet. The tower is 150 feet and is built on a 45-foot bluff.

First Florida Lighthouse Ever Built: St. Augustine Lighthouse (1824)

Oldest Existing Tower: Amelia Island Lighthouse (1839)

Oldest Reef Lighthouse: Carysfort Reef (1852)

Second Oldest Tower: St. Mark's (1842)

First Modern Brick Tower: Dry Tortugas Lighthouse (1858) on Loggerhead Key stands at 150 feet.

Most Towers Built in One Location: Four towers were built at the Cape San Blas Lighthouse from 1847 to 1918.

First Fresnel Lens in Florida: Sand Key Lighthouse was lit on July 20, 1853.

First American Light Station in Florida: St. Augustine Lighthouse became operational on April 5, 1824.

First Navigational Aid in Florida: The British established a day marker at Mosquito Inlet in 1774.

Shortest Lighthouse Tower: Cedar Key Lighthouse, located on Seahorse Key, is 23 feet tall and is located on a 52-foot bluff.

First Lightship: *Aurora Borealis* (1823–25) was stationed off Pensacola.

First West Coast Lighthouse: Pensacola Lighthouse was built in December 1824.

Only Fog Signal: Located at Egmont Key

Last Manned Station: St. Johns River (1954) was automated in 1967.

Lowest Focal Plane: Boca Grande Lighthouse is 41 feet tall.

First Light in the Keys: Cape Florida Lighthouse was lit in December 1825.

Traveling Lighthouse: St. Joseph Point Lighthouse was discontinued in 1960. In 1979, it moved 6 and 23 miles, respectively.

Furthest North: Amelia Island

Furthest South: Sand Key

Furthest East: Fowey Rocks

Furthest West: Pensacola

Designed the Most Lighthouses in the State: General George Meade (6 in total)

Cape Canaveral Light: Located on the Canaveral Air Force Base, where the Mercury, Gemini, and Apollo missions were launched.

Lighthouse Glossary

aid to navigation: Any device external to a vessel or aircraft specifically intended to assist navigators in determining their position or safe course or to warn them of danger or obstructions to navigation

appropriation: An act by the US Congress authorizing money paid from the Treasury for purposes of a specific task, project, or study. A lighthouse project usually required several appropriations before construction could begin.

Argand lamp: Clean-burning oil lamp that was widely used in the Lighthouse Service during the late eighteenth and early nineteenth centuries. The lamp was designed by French inventor Aimé Argand.

assistant keeper: A person or persons who helped a head lighthouse keeper maintain a lighthouse. At the larger lighthouses, especially coastal lights, one or more assistant keepers were required to maintain the light station complex, keep lamps lit, and keep fog signals operating properly.

astragal: An astragal is a type of bead-like molding, which is commonly used to provide a seal between two doors. It also can be used as an ornamental, as in a lighthouse. It protects structures from harsh weather conditions, or it can minimize the passage of light if installed diagonally on glass windows.

candle power: A measure of the lighting intensity of lamps or lighting apparatus used in the lighthouse

characteristic: The identifying light feature of a lighthouse beacon. To help mariners distinguish between different beacons, every location had a distinct color or flashing sequence.

clamshell or bivalve lenses: Most Fresnel lenses are round, but some are flattened, resembling a clamshell or bivalve.

clockworks mechanism: A mechanical device that is similar to a grandfather clock and is used to rotate a beacon or ring a fog bell. The mechanism needed to be manually set every four to six hours to maintain its use.

Coast Guard: Since 1939, lighthouses and other aids to navigation in America have been the responsibility of the US Coast Guard. Prior to the Coast Guard, all aids to navigation were operated by the Lighthouse Service.

day beacon: A beacon or aid to navigation that does include a light

decommissioned light: A lighthouse that no longer functions as an aid to navigation. It is sometimes referred to as an extinguished light.

diaphone: A powerful foghorn invented in Canada that produces a loud blast to warn mariners during periods of low visibility. The foghorn is operated by compressed air generated by a steam, gas, or oil engine.

establish: The date that the light station was completed and the first lighting of the lamp occurred

fixed light: A lighthouse beacon that shines constantly during its regular hours of operation

flashing light: A lighthouse beacon that shows an on and off characteristic at a regular interval

focal plane: The height of the lighthouse lens focal point above sea level

fog bell: A distinct sound signal, usually a horn, trumpet, or siren, used to warn vessels away from prominent headlands or navigational obstructions during fog or periods of low visibility

foghorn: *See* diaphone

Fresnel lens: Invented in 1822 by Augustin Fresnel, a French physicist, the lens consists of a series of glass prisms supported by brass framework. The light reflected through the lenses concentrates the light beam that can be viewed for distances up to 25 miles.

keeper: A person who was responsible for all the operations at a light station. Lighthouse keepers were appointed by the president of the United States or the secretary of the Treasury prior to the Civil War.

Lighthouse Glossary

lamp: The lighting apparatus inside the lens. They vary in type and design, depending how they are powered: oil, kerosene vapor, or electric.

LAMP: Lighthouse Automation Modernization Program was initiated in 1968 and was extended to 1989 to accelerate and standardize the remaining lighthouses for automation

lighthouse: An enclosed tower or building, constructed by the government, and designed to function as an aid to navigation

Light List: An official Coast Guard list of aids to navigation along the coasts and inland waterways, featuring brief descriptions of the aid and precise locations

lightships: Lightships were floating lighthouses that were equipped with their own beacons. The beacons were positioned on a tall central mast. They marked shoals where construction of a lighthouse was impossible or prohibitively expensive.

light station: A navigation facility with a light beacon, commonly referred to as a light or light station. Light stations are often interchanged with lighthouses, but a light station might not include a keeper's quarter or fog signal.

LORAN: Acronym for "Long-Range Navigation Aid." LORAN is an electronic aid to navigation, consisting of a shore-based radio transmitter. The LORAN communication system enables users to determine their position quickly and accurately day or night.

occulting or eclipsing light: There are several ways to produce a beacon that appears to flash. One way is to block (or occult) the light at regular intervals, often with a rotating opaque panel.

pile: A long, heavy timber, iron girder, or concrete post driven into a seabed or riverbed. Piles serve as a support for a lighthouse or other aids to navigation.

range lights: A pattern of navigation lights, usually fixed ashore, help vessels navigate narrow channels, usually at night. They are designed for short- to medium-range directional light to help with port traffic. Most often, they are simple skeleton towers.

riprap: Large stones that are placed around the lighthouse or the foundation to reduce the wave energy and protect against ice damage

screw pile: A specially designed pile that can be screwed into the bottom of the seabed, particularly into coral and rock, for the support of a lighthouse or other aids to navigation

SHORAN: Acronym for "Short-Range Navigation Aid." It is an electronic aid used similar to LORAN.

skeleton tower: Iron or steel skeleton light towers consisting of four or more heavily braced metal legs and topped with a lantern

US Life-Saving Service: The service was established in 1876 by Miles Kimball. Manned stations were set up primarily on ocean waters to rescue boaters from the ocean surf.

US Lighthouse Board: The board was created in 1851 by a group of engineers, scientists, and military personnel who worked to modernize the Lighthouse Service's practices. It served as the board of directors for the US Lighthouse Establishment.

US Lighthouse Establishment: The first official name of the American lighthouse agency. Promoted by President George Washington; Congress passed legislation on August 7, 1789, that created the Lighthouse Establishment. It remained the Lighthouse Establishment until the Bureau of Lighthouses was established within the Department of Commerce and Labor in 1910.

US Lighthouse Service: A common term applied to different organizations that built or maintained the US lighthouses from 1789 until 1939, when the Coast Guard was placed in charge.

Bibliography

Adamson, Hans Christian. *Keepers of the Lights*. New York: Greenberg, 1955.

Barnes, Jay. *Florida's Hurricane History*. Foreword by Steve Lyons. Chapel Hill: University of North Carolina Press, 2007.

Bathurst, Bella. *The Lighthouse Stevensons*. New York: HarperCollins, 1999.

Beaver, Patrick. *A History of Lighthouses*. Secaucus, NJ: Citadel, 1971.

Bingham, Doug. *Lightship Stations of the US Government*. Washington, DC: US Coast Guard, 1989.

Bingham, Doug. US Lightship Station Assignments. http://uscg.mil/history/Lightship_Station_Index.html

Cipra, David. *Lighthouses & Lightships of the Northern Gulf of Mexico*. Washington, DC: US Department of Transportation and US Coast Guard, 1978.

Clark, James C. *A Concise History of Florida*. Charleston, SC: History Press, 2014.

Clifford, Candace. *Nineteenth-Century Lights*. Alexandria, VA: Cypress Communications, 2000.

Clifford, Mary Louise, and J. Candace Clifford. *Women Who Kept the Lights: An Illustrated History of Female Lighthouse Keepers*. Alexandria, VA: Cypress Communications, 1993.

Couch, Ernie, and Jill Couch. *Florida Trivia*. Nashville: Rutledge Hill, 1994.

Crompton, Samuel Willard, and Michael J. Rhein. *The Ultimate Book of Lighthouses*. San Diego, CA: Thunder Bay, 2003.

DeWire, Elinor. *Lighthouse Victuals and Verse*. Gales Ferry, CT: Sentinel, 1996.

DeWire, Elinor. *Sentries along the Shore*. Gales Ferry, CT: Sentinel, 1997.

Florida Atlas and Gazetteer. Yarmouth, ME: DeLorme, 2006.

Fuson, Robert H. *Juan Ponce de León and the Spanish Discovery of Puerto Rico and Florida*. Blacksburg, VA: McDonald & Woodward, 2000.

Gannon, Michael. *Florida: A Short History*. Gainesville: University Press of Florida, 1993.

Gaske, Frederick P., ed. *Florida British Heritage Trail*. Tallahassee: Florida Department of State, Division of Historical Resources, 2014.

Gaultier, Kimberley, Gaël de Maisonneuve, Bruce Graetz, Susanne Hunt, and Philippe Létrilliart, eds. *Florida French Heritage Trail*. Tallahassee: Florida Department of State, Division of Historical Resources, 2014.

Goetzmann, William, and Glyndwr Williams. *The Atlas of North American Exploration*. Norman: University of Oklahoma Press, 1992.

Grown, Robin C. *Florida's First People—12,000 Years of Human History*. Sarasota, FL: Pineapple, 1994.

Hairr, John. *Florida Lighthouses*. Images of America. San Francisco: Arcadia, 1999.

Handy, Amy. *American Landmarks: The Lighthouse*. New York: Smithmark, 1997.

Harrison, Tim. "Accused Lincoln Assassinator Held Here." *Lighthouse Digest*, April 2014.

Harrison, Tim, and Ray Jones. *Lost Lighthouses*. Guilford, CT: Globe Pequot, 2000.

Bibliography

Holland, F. Ross, Jr. *America's Lighthouses: An Illustrated History*. New York: Dover, 1972.

Holland, F. Ross, Jr. *Lighthouses*. New York: Barnes & Noble, 1997.

Hurley, Neil E. *Florida's Lighthouses in the Civil War*. Oakland Park, FL: Middle River, 2007.

Kochel, Kenneth G. *America's Atlantic Coast Lighthouses*. Clearwater, FL: Betken, 1996.

Love, Dean. *Lighthouses of the Florida Keys*. Key West, FL: Historic Florida Keys Foundation, 1992.

McCarthy, Kevin. *Florida Lighthouses*. Gainesville: University of Florida Press, 1994.

McGrath, John T. *The French in Early Florida: In the Eye of the Hurricane*. Gainesville: University of Florida Press, 2000.

Merryman, J. H. *The United States Life-Saving Service—1880*. Silver Thorne, CO: Vista Books, 1997.

Milanich, Jerald T. *Hernando de Soto and the Indians of Florida*. Gainesville: University Press of Florida, 1997.

Neill, Wilfred. *The Story of Florida Seminole Indians*. St. Petersburg, FL: Great Outdoors, 1956.

Nordhoff, Charles. *The Lighthouses of the United States in 1874*. Golden, CO: Outbooks, 1981.

Parkman, Francis. *France and England in North America*. Vol. 1, *Pioneers of France in the New World*. Literary Classics of the United States. New York: Library of America, 1983.

Pleasonton, Stephen. *Instructions for Light-Keepers of the United States*. Washington, DC: US Treasury Department, 1835.

Powell, Jack. *Time Traveler's Guide to Florida*. Sarasota, FL: Pineapple, 2014.

Ricky, Donald B., ed. *The Encyclopedia of Florida Indians: Tribes, Nations, and People of the Woodlands Areas*. 2 vols. St. Clair Shores, MI: Somerset, 1998.

Roberts, Bruce, and Ray Jones. *American Lighthouses: A Definitive Guide*. Old Saybrook, CT: Globe Pequot, 1998.

Roberts, Bruce, and Ray Jones. *Southern Lighthouses*. Old Saybrook, CT: Globe Pequot, 1995.

Shanks, Ralph, and Wick York. *The US Life-Saving Service*. Petaluma, CA: Costano Books, 1997.

Smith, Robert. *Maritime Museums of North America*. Annapolis, MD: Naval Institute Press, 1990.

Snyder, James. *A Light in the Wilderness: The Story of Jupiter Inlet Lighthouse*. Jupiter, FL: Pharos Books, 2014.

Standiford, Les. *Last Train to Paradise: Henry Flagler and the Spectacular Rise and Fall of the Railroad That Crossed an Ocean*. Waterville, ME: Thorndike, 2003.

Stewart, Walter. *The Lighthouses Act of 1789*. Washington, DC: US Senate Historical Office, 1991.

Taylor, Thomas. *Florida Lighthouse Trail*. Sarasota, FL: Pineapple, 2001.

Thompson, Donald, and Carol Thompson. *Egmont Key: A History*. Charleston, SC: History Press, 2012.

Tuers, Rick. *Lighthouses of New York*. Atglen, PA: Schiffer, 2007.

Weiss, George. *The Lighthouse Service: Its History, Activities and Organization*. Baltimore: Johns Hopkins Press, 1926.

Index

Adams, John Quincy, 26, 99

Ais, 26

Alcazar Hotel, 70

Alligator Reef Lighthouse, 81

Amelia Island Lighthouse, 29, 181

Amelia Island North Range Lighthouse, 162

American Shoal Lighthouse, 77, 87

Anclote Key Lighthouse, 11, 113

Andreu, Joseph, 35

Andreu, Juan, 35

Andreu, Maria de los Delores Mestre, 35

Apalachee, 26

Argand, Aimé, 18, 29

Argand lamp, 18, 19, 29, 182

Army Corps of Engineers (*see* US Army Corps of Engineers)

Army Corps of Topographical Engineers, 23, 67, 75, 83

astragal, 90

Baggs, Bill, 64, 65, 67

Baker's Island Lighthouse, 15

Bald Island Lighthouse, 15

Barefoot Mailmen, 59, 63

Barrier Island Parks Society, 121, 123, 125

Beacon Hill Lighthouse, 27, 143, 144

Beavertail Lighthouse, 14

Bethel, Joseph, 95

Bethel, Mary, 95, 97

Bethel, Merrill, 95

Bethel, William, 95, 97

Bill Baggs Cape Florida State Park, 64–65

Biloxi Lighthouse, 106

Biscayne Bay House of Refuge (Miami Beach), 61

Boca Grande Entrance Rear Range Lighthouse, 120–123

Boca Grande Lighthouse, 120, 125

Boca Grande Lighthouse Museum, 125

Bodie Island Lighthouse, 47

Booth, John Wilkes, 101

Boston Lighthouse, 14

Brandt Point Lighthouse, 14

breeches buoy, 60

Bureau of Lighthouses, 183

Burnham, Captain, 47

Caesar Lightship, 75

Calusa, 26, 65

Cape Ann Lighthouse, 14

Cape Canaveral, 26, 47, 49, 51

Cape Canaveral Lighthouse, 43, 46, 47

Cape Canaveral Lighthouse Foundation, 49

Cape Cod Lighthouse, 15

Cape Florida Lighthouse, 73, 75, 181

Cape Hatteras Lighthouse, 15, 34, 36, 41

Cape Haze Lighthouse, 163

Cape Henlopen Lighthouse, 14

Cape Henry Lighthouse, 15

Cape Kennedy Air Force Station, 47

Cape Malabar House of Refuge, 61

Cape San Blas Lighthouse, 128, 139, 181

Cape St. George Lighthouse, 147

Cape St. George Lighthouse Society, 148–151

Carnegie Marine Biology Lab, 105

Carrabelle Lighthouse Association, 154

Carroll, John J., 94

Carroll, Mary, 95

Carysfort Reef Lighthouse, 77, 83, 90, 173

Carysfort Reef Lightship, 45

Cedar Key Historical Society Museum, 111

Cedar Key Lighthouse (Seahorse Key), 111

Cedar Key Museum State Park, 111

Cedar Key National Wildlife Refuge, 111

Charleston Lighthouse, 14

Charlotte Harbor, 120, 125, 163

Charlotte Harbor Lighthouse, 163

Chester Shoal House of Refuge, 61

Choctaws, 26

Churchill, Winston, 57

Cleveland, Grover, 113

Creeks (tribe), 26

Crooked River Lighthouse, 154, 155

Cumberland Island, 29

Cumberland Sound, 29

Index

Dames Point Lighthouse, 45, 164

Dames Point Lightship, 164

Delaware Breakwater Rear Range Light (Green Hill Lighthouse), 121

Dog Island, 153, 165

Dog Island Lighthouse, 153

Doyle, William, 166

Drake, Sir Francis, 73

Dry Tortugas Light (Loggerhead Key), 103, 105

Dry Tortugas National Park, 103

Duck Island, 83

Dudley, Ann, 97

Dutcher, William, 90

Duval, William P., 70, 157

East Gulf Blockading Squadron, 118

Eaton's Neck Lighthouse, 15

Eddystone Lighthouse, 16

Edison, Thomas, 108, 127, 177

Egmont Key Lighthouse, 33, 116–118, 128, 181

Fernandina Beach Harbor, 29, 162

Fine, Sarah, 97

Flagler, Henry, 70, 108, 185, 187

Flaherty, John, 99

Flaherty, Rebecca, 97

Florida East Coast Railway, 70

Florida History Center and Museum, 55

Florida Lighthouse Association, 11, 31, 49, 178

Florida Lightship, 45

Florida Keys National Marine Sanctuary, 87

fog signals, 16, 182

Ford, Henry, 127

Fort Barrancus Rear Range Lighthouse, 166

Fort Dade, 118

Fort Desoto Park, 119

Fort Jefferson Lighthouse (*see* Garden Key Lighthouse)

Fort Jefferson National Monument, 100

Fort McRee Rear Range Lighthouses, 167

Fort Niagara Lighthouse, 14

Fort Pickens Lighthouse, 135, 167

Fort Zachary Taylor, 96

Fowey Rocks Lighthouse, 73

Fresnel, Augustine Jean, 18–20

Fresnel lens, 13, 16, 18–21, 36, 37, 39, 42, 43, 53, 55, 58, 76, 77, 83, 84, 86, 90, 94, 95, 134, 135, 181, 182

Gage, Mark, 173

Gallatin, Albert, 15

Garden Key Lighthouse, 100, 105, 106

Gasparilla Island, 125, 163

Gay Head Lighthouse, 15

Gilberts Bar House of Refuge (or St. Lucie Rocks), 61

global positioning system (GPS), 33, 177

Great Point Lighthouse, 14

Grisham, Alton, 159

Hamilton, Alexander, 8, 14

Henry, John, 22

Hillsboro Lighthouse, 59, 63, 76

Hillsboro Lighthouse Preservation Society, 59

Hillsboro Lighthouse Station, 59

Honey Lightship, 89

Hoover, Herbert, 84

houses of refuge, 60–63

Humphries, Noah, 65

Hungerford, John, 158

Indian River / Bethel Creek House of Refuge, 61

Ingraham, Jeremiah, 97, 134

Ingraham, Michaela, 97

iron-pile lights, 71, 79, 83

Jackson, Andrew, 26, 133, 157

Jannus, Anthony, 108

Johnson, Charles G., 90

Johnson, Lyndon B., 49

Jupiter Inlet Lifesaving Station, 61

Jupiter Inlet Lighthouse, 13, 51, 52, 54, 55

keeper's log, 179

Kennedy, David, 158

Kennedy Space Center, 47

Key Largo, 45, 75, 83, 93, 99

Key West, 13, 70, 87, 91–97, 103, 128, 171, 172

Key West Lighthouse, 84, 92–96

Kimball, Sumner, 61

King George II of England, 29

Knight, Thomas, 57

Koslow, Howard, 106

Florida Lighthouses | 187

Index

La Florida, 26

Lamberton, B. P., 175

LAMP (Lighthouse Automation Modernization Program), 177

Leadbetter, Danville, 23

Lee, Robert E., 23, 83

Lewis, Winslow, 15, 16, 19, 29, 75, 170

lifeboats, 60

life car, 60

Life-Saving Service (see US Life-Saving Service)

Lighthouse Board (see US Lighthouse Board)

Lighthouse Digest, 140, 184

Lighthouse Establishment, 8, 13–15, 183

Lighthouse Point, 57

Lighthouse Preservation Society, 9, 11, 59, 178, 179

Lighthouses of New York, 2, 9, 11

Lightships, 13, 15, 20, 21, 45, 75, 177

Lincoln, Abraham, 101

Lincoln, Samuel B., 93

Little Brewster Island (see Boston Lighthouse)

Little Cumberland Island Lighthouse, 29

Loggerhead Key (see Dry Tortugas)

LORAN (Long-Range Navigation Aids), 17, 33, 183

Loxahatchee River Historical Society, 55

Lyle gun, 60

Mabrity, Barbara, 93, 97

Mabrity, Michael, 93

Mallory Square, 70

Matagorda Island Lighthouse, 106

Matanzas Inlet House of Refuge (see Smith's Creek)

Mayport Lighthouse, 31, 45

Mayport Naval Station, 31, 33

McDonald, Frances, 97

McKinley, William, 143

Meade, George, 23, 41, 50, 51, 67, 75, 83, 90, 110, 111

Menéndez de Avilés, Pedro, 35

Molasses Reef Light, 168

Monroe, President, 26, 133

Montauk Point Lighthouse, 15

Mosquito Inlet Lighthouse (see Ponce Inlet Lighthouse)

Mosquito Lagoon House of Refuge, 61

Mudd, Dr. Samuel A., 101

National Aids to Navigation School, 105

National Naval Aviation Museum, 137

Naval Radio Detection Finding Station, 155

Naval Radio Station, 54

Newbury Lighthouse, 14

New London Lighthouse, 14

New River House of Refuge (Ft. Lauderdale), 61

Northwest Passage Lighthouse, 45, 171

Northwest Passage Lightship, 45, 171

Ocracoke Lighthouse, 15

Oil House Museum, 55

Orange Grove House of Refuge, 63

Overseas Highway, 70, 87

Palmes, Joseph, 134

Penalber, Michaela, 134

Pensacola Lighthouse, 97, 134, 136, 137, 166

Pensacola Lifesaving Station, 62

Perry, Matthew C., 93, 99

Phiel, Abe, 108

Pippin, James L., 36

Plant, Henry B., 108

Plant Museum, 108

Pleasonton, Stephen, 15, 19, 20

Plymouth Lighthouse, 14

Ponce de León, Juan, 99, 133

Ponce Inlet, 12, 43, 61, 170

Ponce Inlet Lighthouse, 21, 43, 44

Port Charlotte, 26, 109

Port Charlotte Lighthouse, 163

Portland Head Lighthouse, 15

Port Pontchartrain, 23

Portsmouth Lighthouse, 14

Pulaski Shoal Lighthouse, 172

Putnam, George R., 16

rapeseed oil, 22

Rebecca Shoal Lighthouse, 77, 173

Renwick, James, 35

Ribault, Jean, 27, 31

Richard C. Callaway Museum, 137

Rikard, George, 118

Ringling, John and Mable, 109

Roosevelt, Franklin D., 100

188 | Florida Lighthouses

Index

Rousseau, Lawrence, 117

Sabin Pass, 23
Sabin Pass Lighthouse, 106
Sambo Keys, 93
Sand Island, 23, 106
Sand Island Lighthouse, 23
Sand Key, 23, 45, 77, 83, 89, 90, 91, 99, 100
Sand Key Lighthouse, 45, 89, 90, 99
Sand Key Lightship, 45
Sandy Hook Lighthouse, 14
Sanibel Historical Village and Museum, 129
Sanibel Island Lighthouse, 128
Santa Rosa Island, 61, 134
Santa Rosa Lifesaving Station, 61
Scott, Rick, 159
screw pile, 16, 73, 183
Seahorse Key, 111, 181
Sequin Lighthouse, 15
SHORAN (Short Range Navigation Aids), 17
Shubrick, William, 16
Simonton, John W., 93
skeleton tower, 16, 23, 73, 127, 140, 144, 183
Smith's Creek House of Refuge, 61
Smyrna Dunes Coast Guard Station, 43
Sombrero Key Lighthouse, 83
Spangler, Edman, 101
Statue of Liberty, 16, 22, 177
St. Augustine, 12, 21, 34–39, 70
St. Augustine Lighthouse, 35, 36, 38, 181

Stiltsville (Key Biscayne), 68
St. Johns Lightship, 31
St. Johns River, 26, 30–33, 45, 97, 164, 174, 175
St. Johns River Lighthouse, 31
St. Joseph Bay Aquatic Preserve, 139
St. Joseph Bay Lighthouse, 143
St. Joseph Point Lighthouse (St. Joseph Light Range Station), 181
St. Marks Lighthouse, 97, 159
St. Marks National Wildlife Refuge, 157, 159
St. Mary's River Inlet, 29, 162
St. Petersburg Museum of History, 108
Strong, Samuel B., 65
surfboat, 60
surfmen, 60–62

Taft, William Howard, 16
Tallahassee–St. Marks Railroad, 158
Tampa Bay Hotel, 108
Tarpon Springs, 113–115
Tequesta, 26, 65
Timucua, 26
Tortugas Harbor Lighthouse, 100
Totten, James, 79
Trinity House, 15
Tybee Lighthouse, 15

US Air Force, 49
US Army Coast Survey, 79
US Army Corps of Engineers, 67, 186

US Fish and Wildlife Refuge, 118, 159
US Life-Saving Service, 60, 61, 183
US Lighthouse Board, 73, 79, 81, 89, 90, 135, 143, 174, 175, 183
US Lighthouse Society, 11, 178, 179

Vackiere, Angelo, 12
Volusia Bar Lighthouse, 174–176

Washington, George, 13–15, 35, 53
whale oil, 22, 29, 35, 93, 134, 136, 177
Whalton, John, 75
Woodbury, Daniel P., 103

Florida Lighthouses | 189

Biographies of Rick and Terri Tuers

Rick is a native of northern New Jersey and has been a photographer for over forty years. Since his youth, he developed a special fascination for coastal and inland aquatic environments. He graduated from New Jersey Institute of Technology in 1977 and had a career in civil and coastal engineering before retiring in 2013.

To photograph over three hundred lighthouses, Rick has taken ferries, kayaked, and hiked countless miles. He has enlisted the help of the US Coast Guard and the Coast Guard Auxiliary throughout New England. For this book on Florida, he has flown over parts of the West Coast and down to Key West to capture the offshore lighthouses.

Rick's special interest in lighthouses has taken him all over the United States, Canada, Mexico, and Italy. In 2007, he published *Lighthouses of New York* (Schiffer Publishing). Rick is an active member of the United States Lighthouse Society and Florida Lighthouse Association. He has published numerous travel articles and presented talks on the lighthouses of New York and New England. He has won several regional photography awards and has been interviewed on National Public Radio and on several television stations in Albany, New York. Besides working as a freelance photographer, Rick travels extensively to photograph lighthouses, wildlife, and landscapes.

Terri is a native of Cleveland, Ohio, and a graduate of Allegheny College (Meadville, Pennsylvania). She is a Renaissance woman who has a science and writing background. She has married both disciplines by working in corporate America and government as a writer and a project manager. She founded two companies, one in public relations / marketing / special events, and another in marketing renewable energy. She was also a freelance writer, producing educational energy curriculum for K–12 and training teachers. She has supported Rick in his creative pursuits while pursuing her own. Appearing on TV and radio talk shows, Terri wrote and produced two documentaries, published many magazine articles, and is currently working on another book.

Together, they share their love of traveling and the great outdoors. They have been to almost all fifty states and are actively checking off world destinations on their "Bucket List," to photograph God's creation and learn about other cultures. They have actively pursued missionary work in Mexico, Zambia, and Bosnia. They are currently helping the poor in Mexico.

All Florida Lighthouses

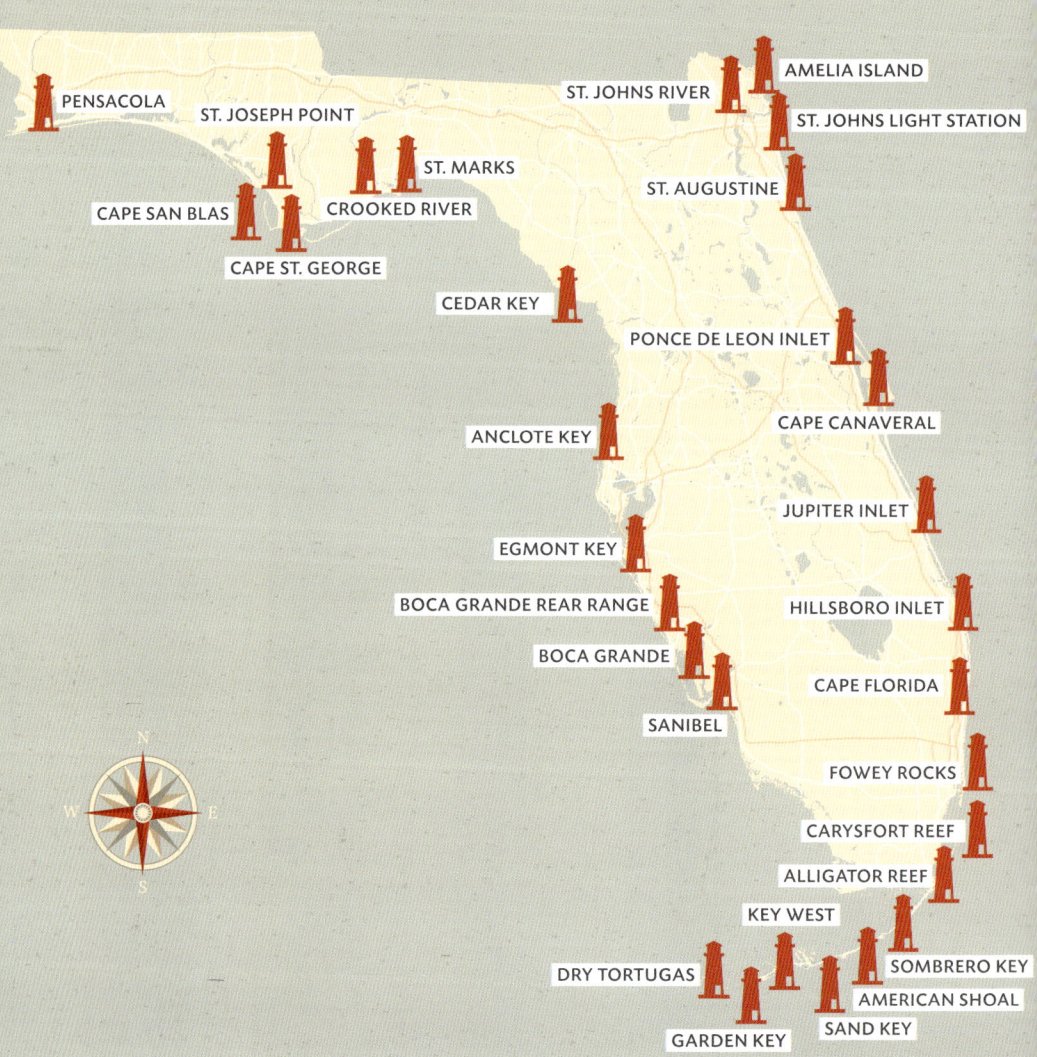